THE EXCELLENCE
OF EXPOSITION

THE EXCELLENCE
OF EXPOSITION

by

DOUGLAS M. WHITE

Foreword by Stephen F. Olford

LOIZEAUX BROTHERS
Neptune, New Jersey

FIRST EDITION, JUNE 1977

Library of Congress Cataloging in Publication Data

White, Douglas Malcolm, 1909-
The excellence of exposition.

Bibliography: p. 179
Includes indexes.
1. Preaching. I. Title.
BV4211.2.W433   251   77-6807
ISBN 0-87213-938-7

191 P.

PRINTED IN THE UNITED STATES OF AMERICA

To

my beloved pastor

CHARLES GRANTLAND FULLER, D. D.

eloquent preacher

and

esteemed friend

CONTENTS

FOREWORD

"Preaching is primary . . . but expository preaching is paramount." This is the thrust of Dr. Douglas M. White's valuable dissertation on *The Excellence of Exposition.* And this emphasis is certainly needed at a time when pulpits have no power, sermons no substance, and preachers — in the words of Ruskin — "play stage tricks with the doctrines of life and death." Of course, there are exceptions; but such will be found only in the churches where ministers adhere strictly to the time-tested art of Word-proclamation. After all, "it is not our comment on the Word that saves, but the Word itself" (R. M. McCheyne); therefore, the preacher must be a mouthpiece for his text, opening it up and applying it as the Word of God in such a manner that the voice of God is heard.

Dr. White, by virtue of his many years of pulpit ministry, his wide experience and diligent research, is eminently qualified to write on *The Excellence of Exposition.* This will become obvious to colleagues in the ministry who read this book. They will find something in these pages to guide, guard, and gladden them in their great task of heralding the gospel of our Lord and Saviour Jesus Christ.

For a number of years now, I have deplored the dearth of expository preaching. By and large, the level of the church's teaching and preaching ministry is abysmal. As evangelicals, who hold a high view of Scripture, we should be ashamed of ourselves; for of all people, we should be the most conscientious in our exposition of the Word of God. No greater responsibility has ever been entrusted to the sons of men, and no greater potentiality has been invested in the church on earth. For as R. H. Fuller has observed, "In preaching, God speaks, God acts, God produces faith . . . God revives the church." And surely there is nothing more urgently needed in these distressing days than a Heaven-sent revival! On the other hand, I concur with D. Martyn Lloyd-Jones who reminds us in his book, *Preachers and Preaching,* that "the decadent periods in church history have always been those periods when preaching has declined."

So I welcome and commend this volume with enthusiasm and the earnest prayer that the Holy Spirit would graciously use it to fill our pulpits with anointed expositors of "the living and abiding Word of God."

STEPHEN F. OLFORD

Minister-at-Large
Encounter Ministries
Holmes Beach, Florida

PREFACE

The original volume entitled, *He Expounded,* was released in 1952. A new generation of preachers is now on the scene and many are asking where they might obtain a copy of that book. This has led to a complete revision of the manuscript. The volume has been considerably enlarged, much new material has been included, and a great deal of change has been made in what remains of the former publication.

Hopefully, the experience and research of the past twenty-five years has made it possible for the author to present a much more helpful resource book on the all-important matter of expository preaching. This preacher is more convinced than ever that expository preaching is the most vital and valuable type of pulpit ministry. Having recently completed more than twenty-five years in the same church I am sure that it could not have been done without a major emphasis upon this type of preaching. I feel confident that the congregation would concur with this conclusion also.

The chief concern of this volume is to provide

practical assistance in the matter of procedure, to those who aspire to become proficient in this area of ministry. We pray that their number may be greatly increased.

I would like to express my appreciation to Mrs. Margie Hall, of Bassett, Virginia, for typing the manuscript for me.

D. M. WHITE

Roanoke, Virginia

PART ONE

A PLEA

FOR EXPOSITORY PREACHING

CHAPTER 1

THE ORIGIN OF EXPOSITION

It pleased God by . . . preaching to save them that
believe (1 Corinthians 1:21). God . . . hath . . . manifested His word through preaching (Titus 1:3).

PREACHING IS PRIMARY. Though this is a
positive and dogmatic assertion, there is no hesitation in stating such a premise, because divine revelation, history, and Christian experience all combine
to corroborate it.

Recognizing the fact that there are many ways of
reaching human hearts, and with no thought of
belittling or discrediting the least of them, it can still
be factually maintained that *preaching is primary.*

Though Paul himself counseled that we should
"by *all means* save some," he nevertheless taught and
evidenced in his own ministry that *preaching is
primary,* and all other means must be secondary and
supplemental. When other means have become primary the Church has suffered as a result.

This being true, preaching should have first consideration in our present-day ministry. Sad to say

this is too often untrue. The preparation and presentation of God's message deserves the very best that can be given to it, under the direction of God. It demands every ounce of energy, every atom of intelligence, every shade of talent, every gleam of personality, every emotion of the entire being, in full and utter consecration to God. Everything else must be subsidiary, and must be made to recognize and contribute to the superiority of preaching. Preaching must have priority over all other ministerial functions if it is to glorify God and fulfill the purpose for which it was ordained.

Again, it is our firm and studied conviction that, in the light of the fact that preaching is primary, the style or method known as *expository* preaching is paramount, and will enable the minister to magnify his office more nobly and efficiently than any other method. This and other conclusions expressed in these pages are not merely the private opinions of the author, but have been substantiated by the testimony of Christian leaders through the centuries, as well as by evangelical contemporaries.

EVIDENCES FROM THE OLD TESTAMENT

Expository preaching dates at least as far back as Ezra, the scribe. Dr. Robert Lewis Dabney says:

> It was under Ezra that preaching assumed, by appointment, more nearly its modern place as a constant part of worship, and also its modern character, as an exposition of the written Scriptures.

And all the people gathered themselves together as one man into the street that was before the water gate; and they spake unto Ezra the scribe to bring the book of the law of Moses, which the LORD had commanded to Israel. And Ezra the priest brought the law before the congregation both of men and women, and all that could hear with understanding, upon the first day of the seventh month. And he read therein before the street that was before the water gate from the morning until midday, before the men and the women, and those that could understand; and the ears of all the people were attentive unto the book of the law. And Ezra the scribe stood upon a pulpit of wood, which they had made for the purpose. . . . And Ezra opened the book in the sight of all the people; (for he was above all the people;) and when he opened it, all the people stood up: And Ezra blessed the LORD, the great God. . . . So they read in the book in the law of God distinctly, and gave the sense, and caused them to understand the reading (Nehemiah 8:1-8).

We shall seek in vain for a more apt and scriptural definition of the preacher's work than is contained in these words. Henceforth, as the Jewish antiquaries tell us, "expository preaching prevailed as a regular exercise, following the reading of the Scriptures in the services of the synagogues."

In Nehemiah 9 we read that "they stood up in their place, and read in the book of the law of the LORD their God one fourth part of the day" (9:3). The remainder of the chapter is given over to a historical exposition of the mercy and goodness of God to Israel in days past. These are typical illustrations of preaching in Old Testament times. It seems to have been the method employed throughout the centuries prior to the coming of the Christ, and—though corrupted with tradition and spiritual blindness, and thus lacking authority and power—was still in vogue when Jesus entered His public ministry.

Much more could be said, and perhaps profitably, on the matter of expositional preaching in the Old Testament; but since ours is distinctly a New Testament ministry, it seems necessary only to set forth a precedent and example to show that it is not an innovation, but rather the accepted manner of procedure followed by the minister of the Lord in all preceding generations.

EVIDENCES FROM THE NEW TESTAMENT

It goes without saying that Jesus Christ was superior to all expositors. Though His manner and doctrine were in many cases directly opposite to those which prevailed, He adopted the customary method of reading and expounding the Scriptures. Whether in the synagogue, in the home, on the hillside, in the prow of a boat, or whatever the location, He preached to the people. Publicly and privately He opened the Scriptures for their understanding.

> And they went into Capernaum; and straightway on the sabbath day He entered into the synagogue, and taught. And they were astonished at His doctrine: for He taught them as one that had authority, and not as the scribes (Mark 1:21-22).
> And again He entered into Capernaum after

some days; and it was noised that He was in the house. And straightway many were gathered together, insomuch that there was no room to receive them, no, not so much as about the door: *and He preached the word unto them* (Mark 2:1-2).

And when they were alone, He expounded all things to His disciples (Mark 4:34).

One thing which distinguished Jesus from the scribes of His day, in His teaching and preaching, was the fact that He "spake with authority." His was no cursory, mechanical repetition, but a powerful, heart-searching interpretation and application of the truth, designed to convince His hearers of their need of a personal relationship to God through Him, and of His right to claim their faith and allegiance for Himself. He did not have to preach to empty pews. People will come to hear the Scriptures preached, even if it is offensive to their pride (as much of His preaching was), when it bears the stamp of divine approval and has the ring of heavenly authority.

"When they were alone, He expounded all things to His disciples" (Mark 4:34). The deeper things, beyond the comprehension of the populace, held the apostles spellbound, as He expounded them to His followers in private. Wuest says that the word "expounded" literally means "to give additional loosening," so as to explain, make plainer and clearer, the Word of God.

Possibly the most notable example of public exposition on the part of Jesus is recorded in Luke 4:16-22:

And He came to Nazareth, where He had been
brought up: and, as His custom was, He went into
the synagogue on the sabbath day, and stood up for
to read. And there was delivered unto Him the book
of the prophet Esaias. And when He had opened the
book, He found the place where it was written, The
Spirit of the Lord is upon Me, because He hath
anointed Me to preach the gospel to the poor; He
hath sent Me to heal the brokenhearted, to preach
deliverance to the captives, and recovering of sight
to the blind, to set at liberty them that are bruised,
To preach the acceptable year of the Lord. And He
closed the book, and He gave it again to the
minister, and sat down. And the eyes of all them
that were in the synagogue were fastened on Him.
And He began to say unto them, This day is this
scripture fulfilled in your ears. And all bare Him
witness, and wondered at the gracious words which
proceeded out of His mouth.

Though He read only two verses from Isaiah 61, it
is quite possible, even probable, that He gave them
an extended exposition of those statements in their
context. Only what He "began to say unto them" is
recorded for us; with the consequent result that the
people "wondered [were filled with wonder] at the
gracious words which proceeded out of His mouth."
That was exposition at its best. Something of the
practical results from this kind of exposition done by
our Lord is set forth in the experience of the Em-
maus disciples.

Then He said unto them, O fools, and slow of
heart to believe all that the prophets have spoken:
Ought not Christ to have suffered these things, and

to enter into His glory? And beginning at Moses and all the prophets, He expounded unto them in all the scriptures the things concerning Himself. . . . And they said one to another, Did not our heart burn within us, while He talked with us by the way, and while He opened to us the scriptures? And they rose up the same hour, and returned to Jerusalem, and found the eleven gathered together, and them that were with them, Saying, The Lord is risen indeed (Luke 24:25-27,32-34).

It was as "He expounded unto them in all the scriptures the things concerning Himself" that these discouraged, heavyhearted disciples found their hearts to "burn within" them; and it was this opening of the Scriptures to the eyes of their understanding which sent them back to the city that same night with a glowing testimony of a renewed faith.

Luke shows in his second treatise that the apostolic Church leaders followed the same pattern of preaching as exemplified by Jesus. The first gospel message delivered by Peter on the day of Pentecost is an exposition of passages from the prophecy of Joel and from the book of Psalms. Of course, it must be remembered that New Testament preaching was not only declarative exposition, but also involved the introduction of new revelation, which is not true of present-day preaching; and therefore is not strictly exemplary in every respect, though the principles are identical.

Stephen's address (Acts 7) is an expository dissertation covering the historical portions of Genesis and

Exodus, along with a brief summary of the Babylonian captivity, with a very pungent application to that generation.

Philip follows the same procedure in dealing with the Ethiopian (Acts 8:26-35), giving him an exposition of Isaiah 53: "and began at the same scripture and preached unto him Jesus" (verse 35).

Second only to Jesus Christ Himself as an expositor there is the Apostle Paul.

> They came to Thessalonica, where was a synagogue of the Jews: And Paul, as his manner was, went in unto them, and three sabbath days reasoned with them out of the scriptures, Opening and alleging, that Christ must needs have suffered, and risen again from the dead; and that this Jesus, whom I preach unto you, is Christ (Acts 17:1-3).

"As his manner was" depicts the characteristic method of Paul, which was that of the expositor. In that same chapter (verses 10-12), we find that such preaching caused the more sincere Bereans to make a personal study of the Scriptures for themselves, which in turn resulted in their belief of the gospel unto salvation.

> And when they had appointed him a day, there came many to him into his lodging; to whom he expounded and testified the kingdom of God, persuading them concerning Jesus, both out of the law of Moses, and out of the prophets (Acts 28:23).

At the close of his long and fruitful ministry, when the apostle was enduring his last confinement before execution, we find that experience had in no wise caused Paul to depart from the expository method which evidently had proved to be most beneficial.

That Paul esteemed the expository method above all others is further revealed in his counsel to Timothy, his young son in the faith and in the ministry: "Until I come give constant attention to the public reading of the Scriptures, to personal appeals, to exposition" (1 Timothy 4:13 Way).

This very clearly calls for the expositional treatment of passages of Scripture, presented in such a way as to obtain a favorable reaction from the listeners. In this way the hearers are indoctrinated with the truths of divine revelation, and must necessarily face the claims disposed therein. "Study to show thyself approved unto God, a workman that needeth not to be ashamed, rightly dividing the word of truth" (2 Timothy 2:15).

The phrase "rightly dividing the word of truth" is a little difficult to put into English. It has been translated "handling aright the word of truth," "declaring the word of truth without distortion," "rightly administering the word of truth," "cut the word of truth straight," "holding a straight course in the truth," "rightly laying out the word," "giving the true word in the right way," "right handling and skilfully teaching the word of truth." The New Standard Bible Dictionary defines the word "divide" as follows: "The skilful application of parts or aspects of the truth adapted to affect persons specially in need of instruction."

The closing definition seems to be a correct summary of all the various shades of meaning expressed by these scholars. The following pithy comments from some other scholars are right in line with this main thought.

"Giving to each person, occasion, or situation, what is needed—the appropriate truth from His Word" (Author not known).

"What is intended here is not dividing Scripture from Scripture, but teaching Scripture accurately" (Vine).

"Dividing the Word is a metaphor taken from a father or steward cutting and distributing bread among his children" *(Preacher's Homiletic Commentary)*.

The latter would fit right in with the counsel of Jesus: "Who then is the faithful and thoughtful slave, whom his master put in charge of his household, to deal out to the members of it their supplies at the proper time? Blessed [happy] is that slave if, when his master comes back, he finds him so doing" (Matthew 24:45-46 Williams).

Cutting, ploughing, road-building, distributing —all of these seem to be involved. The idea is to go through the Word, without deviation and turning to one side, setting forth what is found therein (whether palatable or not) as it obviously fits the local and present situation; applying the truth in a practical manner to the needs of the hearers, so that it may produce the results for which it is designed.

As a properly trained dietician knows how to

prepare and serve a balanced and nutritious meal, so the diligent and properly enlightened minister is able to edify the Church as well as to instruct the unbeliever.

How could the minister more aptly follow this advice than by a consecutive treatment of the Word of God, chapter by chapter, and book by book?

That minister who has thoroughly prepared himself and is proficient in the realm of exposition is going to be in a position to provide the "household of faith" with that which is most needed and most beneficial at any given time in any place. He will have the unreserved approval of divine authority stamped upon his ministry, and will have no need for apologies or cause for embarrassment.

The apostle's last word on the matter is:

Continue thou in the things which thou hast learned and hast been assured of, knowing of whom thou hast learned them; And that from a child thou hast known the holy scriptures, which are able to make thee wise unto salvation through faith which is in Christ Jesus. All scripture is given by inspiration of God, and is profitable for doctrine, for reproof, for correction, for instruction in righteousness: That the man of God may be perfect, throughly furnished unto all good works. I charge thee therefore before God, and the Lord Jesus Christ, who shall judge the quick and the dead at His appearing and His kingdom; Preach the word; be instant in season, out of season; reprove, rebuke, exhort with all longsuffering and doctrine. For the time will come when they will not endure sound doctrine . . . they shall turn away their ears from the truth . . . make full proof of thy ministry (2 Timothy 3:14 — 4:5).

That is final. The charge is based upon the intrinsic value of the Scriptures themselves, and is followed with the frank acknowledgment that such preaching will not always be popular, but nevertheless expedient and fruitful.

The Scriptures will, first of all, activate the heart and life of the minister himself and then, as he expounds them to others, will have the same effect upon those who heed the message.

The heart and core of the whole passage, the charge itself, is stated in three pertinent and powerful words: *"Preach the word."* Taken in the light of the context it could mean nothing less than expository preaching. Many men are spoken of as preaching the Word because the content of their sermons is quite orthodox and in keeping with divine truth (as all sermons should be), but the challenge of the apostle can be literally carried out only by employing the expositional method. The following brief article sums up the matter most satisfactorily:

> Three out of the twenty-seven books of the New Testament are labeled pastorals. They are so called because Paul, the great apostle to the Gentiles, addressed them to two of his younger friends, Timothy and Titus, who were pastors. In these short but vital letters is found exceedingly valuable advice for pastors all down the centuries. Among the admonitions given is a terse suggestion that we "preach the word." The original term used in the New Testament is *karusso,* which means to cry out, herald, or exhort. It is as if the message so burned in one's heart that it must be expressed with passionate feeling and godly fervor. This is the work of a pastor,

but the pastor is to cry out the Word; that is, his sermons are to be made up of Scripture, not about the Scripture, but the very Word of God itself.

At this point lies the secret of preaching successfully. Godly men, with rare insight into the truth of God, have declared that expository preaching is the thing. If one desires the blessing of God to come upon his congregation, his method of preaching must be to take the Word itself and 'expose' his people to it. Of necessity this must rule out many beautifully turned and highly polished sermons which tickle the ears of the listener. But if there is substituted instead the preaching of the Word of God, it will accomplish God's purpose.

Peter also has some sound advice for us in this respect. "Feed the flock of God" (1 Peter 5:2). The lambs must be nurtured on the "sincere [undiluted] milk of the word" (1 Peter 2:2) until they mature into full-grown sheep. Only the expositional method of preaching will develop a strong, healthy, and well-nourished flock. After all, the only thing that has the authority and guaranteed backing of God is His own Word.

So shall My word be . . . it shall accomplish . . . and it shall prosper (Isaiah 55:11).

Is not My word . . . like a hammer that breaketh the rock in pieces? (Jeremiah 23:29)

The word of God is quick, and powerful [life-giving and wonder-working], and sharper than any twoedged sword (Hebrews 4:12).

The Word of God is the only thing that is guaranteed to shatter Satanic opposition to His will.

His Word is the divine scalpel that pierces through the outer tissues of unbelief, exposing the heart to the healing and disinfecting rays of God's grace. His Word is the only thing that can accomplish His purpose in and for sinful men, and bring prosperity to the soul. "The entrance of Thy words giveth light" (Psalm 119:130).

It would appear that the apostle had the expositional method of preaching in mind when he made his request to the Christians in Thessalonica: "Brethren, pray for us, [not that we may be great preachers but] that the word of the Lord may have free course, and be glorified" (2 Thessalonians 3:1).

CHAPTER 2

THE PROGRESS OF EXPOSITION

FROM PAUL TO PAPACY

THERE IS LITTLE DOUBT that the expositional method of preaching was used almost exclusively in apostolic times. Jesus Christ was, of course, the prince of expositors. However, Paul followed hard in His footsteps, as did the apostles and leaders of the early Church. There is abundant evidence in the book of Acts to show that exposition was the accepted method of imparting divine truth; and I am sure that Timothy, Titus, Crescens, Luke, and John Mark, with many other of their contemporaries, followed the example and advice of the apostle whom they loved, and to whom they owed so much in the spiritual realm.

There does not seem to be a great deal of information left to us concerning the methods of preaching employed in the first three or four centuries, but the scholars are pretty well agreed that the expositional type of ministry prevailed, with a general adherence to the tenets of evangelical Christianity.

"After preaching ceased to be what it was in the mouths of the apostles, a message, properly so called, it became an exposition of the Word of God, of the apostolic writings, of their doctrine, and an application to the silent and assembled flock, of all which had just been read" (Herder).

"In the early church exposition . . . was the rule, and discourses upon set topics and brief texts were the exceptions" (Kidder).

The two renowned preachers of the early centuries (Augustine and Chrysostom) left volumes of expository messages on Genesis, Psalms, Matthew, John, the Pauline Epistles, and many other books of the Bible. There can be no doubt that the expository method was predominant for at least twelve centuries.

"Textual preaching began in the beginning of the thirteenth century" (Dr. J. W. Alexander).

"Expository preaching was used almost exclusively until the thirteenth century" (Dr. T. Harwood Pattison).

In speaking of textual preaching, which has become so increasingly prevalent in the latter centuries, Dr. Austin Phelps says: "For the first twelve Christian centuries there seems to have been no such prevailing habit."

Just as the decline of the spiritual life of the Church was gradual so, doubtless, was the departure from the apostolic method of preaching. As the distinction between church and state diminished, and as ritualism, tradition, and superstition increased (bringing about the papal system which obtains today), so the distinction between church and the world decreased. As the Bible ceased to be recognized as the final authority in all matters pertaining to religion, and more and more authority was claimed by the Pope and ecclesiasticism, the apostolic polity of the church waned. Instead of following, without hesitation, the Biblical order of preaching, and the precedent set by the apostles, ministers began to adopt methods of their own devising, which would be designed to acceptance by the congregations to which they ministered, but without the authority and power of the Holy Spirit.

It could not have happened overnight, but it is highly significant that the wholesale departure from expository to textual preaching was followed by the spiritual eclipse known as the Dark Ages.

To say there was *no* expository preaching, or other good Biblical preaching, during those years would be utterly unreasonable. Nevertheless, the preponderance of the weaker type of ministry gave no opportunity for the expositional type to prevail. Erasmus seems to have recognized this weakness, as evidenced in his counsel to ministerial students:

To get at the real meaning it is not enough to take four or five isolated words; you must look where they came from, what was said, by whom it was said, to whom it was said; at what time, on what occasion, in what words, what preceded, and what follows.

There can be no doubt whatever that the departure from expositional preaching played a very prominent part in promoting the spiritual blindness and darkness of those centuries.

FROM LUTHER TO LETHARGY

The converse is also true. The chief characteristic of that period, which we call the Reformation, was the *return* to expositional preaching.

When the light of divine truth began to emerge from its long eclipse, at the Reformation, there were few things more remarkable than the universal return of evangelicals to the expository method (Alexander).

The topical preaching of Moody moved two continents for Christ; the textual sermons of Spurgeon started movements which are still blessing humanity; but it was the expositions of Luther that redeemed Christendom from the Dark Ages, and instituted the Reformation (Dr. R. B. Jones).

It was a revival of *Biblical* preaching. Instead of long and often fabulous stories about saints and martyrs, and accounts of miracles . . . these men preached the Bible. The question was not what the Pope said; and even the Fathers, however highly esteemed, were not decisive authority—it was the Bible. The preacher's one great task was to set forth the doctrinal and moral teachings of the Word of God. And the greater part of their preaching was *expository*. Once more, after long centuries, people were reading the Scriptures in their own tongue, and preachers . . . were carefully explaining to the people the connected teachings of passage after passage, and book after book. For example, Zwingli . . . announced his intention to preach, not simply upon the church lessons, but upon the whole Gospel of Matthew, chapter after chapter. Some friends objected that it would be an innovation, and injurious; but he justly said, 'It is the old custom. Call to mind the homilies of Chrysostom on Matthew, and of Augustine on John.' There was also at the basis of this expository preaching by the Reformers a much more strict and reasonable exegesis than had ever been common since the days of Chrysostom.

Such careful and continued exposition of the Bible, based in the main upon sound exegesis, and pursued with loving zeal, could not fail of great results, especially at a time when direct and exact knowledge of Scripture was a most attractive and refreshing novelty (Dr. John A. Broadus).

New Testament preaching came into its own once again, with such renowned expositors as Luther and Calvin setting the pace. Nevertheless, the prevalence of expositional preaching was comparatively short-lived. History has been repeating itself. The process has been slow, even as before, but the departure has been just about as widespread as before. Along with it has come a multitude of cults, and other Satanic, subversive influences. The departure has been far more noticeable during the last two centuries, with a terrific slump since the turn of the century in which we are living. This fact, undoubtedly, accounts for the spiritually anemic condition of the Church universal; the widespread apostasy in territories where the gospel has been preached (i.e., Germany —the homeland of Luther); and the tremendous inroad of cults and false religions in all parts of the world.

The absence of expository preaching today is positively alarming.

> We come down to our own times; in which, within our immediate knowledge, there are not a dozen ministers who make the expounding of the Scriptures any part of their stated pulpit exercises (Alexander 1860).

That statement was made over one hundred years ago. If that be true then, how much greater is this failure in our present day?

In the light of that deplorable fact, Alexander makes a passionate plea, one which is most applicable to our own times:

> I would urge that the expository method (understood as that which explains extended passages of Scripture in course) be restored to that equal place which it held in the primitive and reformed churches; for, first, this is obviously the only natural and efficient way to do that which is the sole legitimate end of preaching, to convey the whole message of God to the people.

About thirty years ago a statement appeared in a book review which was an appraisal of a book of expository messages:

> Expository preaching is one of the most profitable forms of unfolding the truth of God's Word. It is far too little used by modern preachers.

Dr. D. P. Kidder has written:

It must be conceded that expository preaching
has been too much neglected of late years, and yet
its primary importance must be perceived by
everyone who will reflect upon its special design to
make the Word of God better understood.

Written in the last century, that appeal is more
urgently needed today than in the day that it was ut-
tered. Dr. H. Jeffs is most emphatic about the matter, almost vituperative in his statements, but we
believe he speaks with real authority:

The Bible is the preacher's book and the
preacher's glory. Bible exposition is the preacher's
main business. If he cannot or will not expound the
Bible, what right has he in any pulpit? He is a
cumberer of the ground that might be occupied by
a fruit-bearing and soul-nourishing tree. If he does
not expound the Bible, what else is there for him to
do? He may deliver addresses out of his own head on
any subject that occurs to him, and may do it well,
but why do it in the pulpit? Is it his own gospel, or
has he a gospel that can just as well be preached
without the Bible, as with it? He is presumably a
preacher of a Christian church, but there would
have been no Christian church today if there had
been no Bible. So long as there remains the triple
tragedy of sin, suffering, and death, so long the
Bible will speak to the heart of man, and humanity
that has once known the Bible, will turn away, after
the novelty has worn off, from every flashy
substitute for the Bible that our modern Athenians
push as the latest thing in the spiritual market.

Finally, this word from a European of a former generation:

> It is to be desired that this kind of preaching were more general. We would have a consecutive exposition of the Word of God, and not a tissue of human reasonings to which the test is accommodated. The discourses of the Fathers of the Church were homilies. Homilies made in good taste, and by men capable of making them, would be extremely useful. We take a passage of Scripture and explain it in its connection; we unfold its interior sense; a multitude of ideas enter, and come, as it were in file; a number of duties are explained in few words. It is a way of preaching more pithy, more scriptural, more Christian. We thus teach the people how to read the Scriptures; we explain it to them; we show the connection between ideas which at first seemed to have little relation to each other. We also adhere more closely to the true Word of God (Dutoit Membrini).

The word "homily" was synonymous with exposition.

Without a doubt we are forced to this necessary conclusion: There has been a wholesale departure from the expository method in this generation which is most deplorable. Certainly the earnest pleas of the well-informed leaders and divines of former generations should come to our ears and hearts with renewed emphasis and appeal, as we view the resultant spiritual decline so evident on every hand in the ranks of Christendom.

Dr. W. Graham Scroggie emphatically declares,

"When the pulpit returns to scholarly, passionate, expository preaching, the pews will again be full." It is at least worth trying.

Since World War Two the trend has been more alarming than ever. It is a rare thing to hear a real expository sermon in the churches any more. In fact a genuine Biblical sermon is conspicuous by its absence. The author is constantly looking forward to a Biblical treat when he is on vacation, and seldom is he rewarded with such. It is a disappointing experience to go away with high hopes and come home empty. Yet this has happened time and again, even when he went out of his way to hear a preacher of repute. It is with genuine regret that one has to make such an acknowledgment. We wish it were not so.

CHAPTER 3

THE APPRAISAL OF EXPOSITION

OBJECTIONS

THOUGH THE MAJORITY of homiletics professors, as well as preachers, extol the expository method and deplore the lack of its use in the pulpit today, there have been some definite objections raised to the extensive employment of expositional preaching. It would be well to consider those objections which may seem to indicate that exposition would be unwise under the conditions which maintain today.

A Lack of Labor

Many are prejudiced toward exposition because they consider it to be a laborsaving device. That is, it becomes a substitute to fall back on in an emergency. That may be due to the fact that the preacher has failed to give adequate time to preparation or, as Broadus puts it:

On rainy Sundays, or on week-nights, the preacher who has no sermon prepared, or wishes to save his elaborate preparation for a more auspicious occasion, will frequently undertake to "read a passage of Scripture and make a few remarks," feeling that this enterprise is attended by no risks because, as some quaint old preacher expressed it, if he is "persecuted in one verse he can flee to another." Hence the people rather naturally conclude that whenever one takes a long text it is an expedient to dispense with labor.

Dr. R. Ames Montgomery also expatiates on this point in a very positive manner:

There seems to be in the minds of some people the idea that expository preaching is an indulgence that a preacher allows himself when the pressure of other things has been encountered. Some lazy men have imagined that they make amends for their neglect and self-indulgence in preparation by what they call expository preaching. Selecting a passage of the Scriptures, they chatter away for half an hour in anecdotal talks suggested by the passage selected. They may try to dignify their action and ease their conscience by calling this expository preaching. It is nothing of the kind.

This gives a distorted idea of exposition, which is naturally considered rather dry, but in no way justifies, though it gives rise to, the prejudice. It may be acknowledged that expository preaching is dry, if the *preacher* is dry. We are quite willing to concede that, but it will also be true of other methods.

This objection will be easily overcome if the

preacher will diligently set himself to excel in the realm of exposition. The fact of the business is that, far from being a laborsaving device, it involves far more laborious effort on the part of the preacher than any other type, as we shall see later on.

A Lack of Bibles

Another objection is that the vast majority of most congregations never carry Bibles to church (a lamentable fact), and thus are not able to follow the trend of thought as it is being developed from the passage under consideration.

The probability is that the people either discontinued the practice of carrying Bibles along to the worship service, or never cultivated it, simply because they found no need for it. This objection constitutes both a challenge and an opportunity. If it is true that this condition exists (and it does), it is due to the fact that the people have never been educated to appreciate the values of exposition. Therefore, when they have been taught to love the fertility and relish the vitality of exposition we shall have overcome the deficiency. There will come about a realization that the hour of worship is not complete without the open Bible before them, which is a most desirable result.

We have enjoyed the most exhilarating experience of beginning a pastorate with possibly only one or two Bibles in the hands of the parishioners and, in a comparatively short length of time (after announcing the chapter), having to wait a few seconds for the rustling of the leaves to subside before continuing. What a heavenly disturbance!

A business man came to our town from another state. He attended some other churches before coming to ours. When the Scripture passage was announced he said that he became aware of a rustling sound, as he turned to the chapter in his own Bible. When he looked around he saw that nearly all the people were turning the leaves of their Bible to find the place. He said that he whispered to his wife: "This is where we belong." He had come from a church where they were accustomed to a Biblical ministry in the pulpit, and this was what they had been looking for.

A Lack of Knowledge

Right along this same line is another objection, that there is such a widespread ignorance of Bible truth and interest in the same. A modern congregation is not disposed to show any depth of appreciation for exposition. Again, we are forced to acknowledge the correctness of the indictment. At the same time, this lack of knowledge is largely due to the fact that the pulpit has failed to instruct the people and thereby stimulate such an interest and desire for Biblical knowledge and understanding. Once more it would seem that such a condition provokes a challenge and an opportunity. Do not say that it *cannot* be done until you have given it a fair trial, over an extended period of time. The fact is it *can* be done. Dr. Jones is right when he says:

> I believe that it can be truthfully said that expository preaching, if wisely done and persistently practiced, will engender such a regard for the Bible in the hearts of the people that they will not be satisfied with any other kind of preaching.

Dr. Phelps tells of a minister in Brooklyn who specialized in expository preaching with very satisfactory results:

> He had trained his inventive power to act in devising methods of making the Bible interesting. He had at command an inexhaustible fund of Biblical information. In his sermons he would career over an entire Biblical chapter with such exhilarating comment, that, in the result, *he carried the audience with him to the end of an hour without a moment of weariness.* He made exegetical learning kindle with oratorical fire.

A Lack of Variety

A further objection, which is shared by many ministers, is that exposition is greatly lacking in variety of content. The lack of real foundation for this objection will be seen in the next chapter.

This is a restless, streamlined age in which we live. There is a tendency to want everything (even sermons) to be condensed, processed, vitaminized, and issued in sugar-coated capsules, along with a glass of lukewarm water. The constant reference to the same book of the Bible each Sunday becomes monotonous, and the necessity of having to concentrate is annoying. It is much more convenient and entertaining if the preacher will merely announce a text as a point of embarkation, and then go on a human interest cruise with something fresh and up-to-date, a resume of the news, a book review, or just a relation of incidents, humorous and otherwise.

This preference is the fruitage of diluted and threadbare pulpit ministry. When an appetite for real Biblical preaching is created, the people will look forward to the next chapter or portion with earnest expectation. They will read in advance and with enthusiasm the Scripture which is to be treated the following Sunday, anticipating the rich treasures which are to be unfolded at the next service. A great deal of disloyalty will be eliminated in this way also, because the people will feel that they are going to suffer much loss if they miss a single message in the series.

The author delivered a series of expository sermons on the book of Second Chronicles which covered the best part of a year. He was quite encouraged when a young woman approached him near the conclusion of the series, and said: "I hope you have another book of the Bible in mind to start on as soon as this one is finished. This is the kind of preaching that does me good."

Some have thought that the well-organized Sunday school has dispensed with the need for expositional preaching, but that is not the case. The Sunday school teacher, even at his best, never presumes to be able to substitute for the expositor, but seeks only to whet the appetite for a heart-warming exposition of the Word in the worship service. Your Sunday school teachers will be your most appreciative listeners. Perhaps the reason that so many leave the church after Sunday school is because they feel that the lesson is superior to the sermon, due to the fact that the teacher stayed with the Scriptures, while the minister merely meandered.

It is extremely doubtful if any concrete objection can be offered to discredit the value and excellence of exposition, if administered under the direction and inspiration of the Holy Spirit.

If "variety is the spice of life," then the expository method, particularly consecutive exposition, will rescue our pulpit menu from the monotonous cycle of soup to hash, and will provide a well-seasoned and well-balanced meal at every sitting.

VIRTUES

The virtues or advantages of expositional preaching stand out in stark contrast to the objections.

Divine Revelation

The Bible is simply a written revelation of God Himself, given to men for the purpose of enlightening their minds concerning His loving purposes and eternal plans for them. Thus preaching is seen to be the divinely appointed means whereby God would work through those whom He has commissioned to be His ministers, in order to impart that truth to men everywhere. Therefore, the expositional method is, obviously, the most proficient way of unfolding this divinely revealed message to men.

Dr. Kidder quotes Thomas Jackson as saying:

> The most useful kind of preaching, we think, is the expository, giving the just meaning of God's own Word, and applying it to the consciences of the people, so as to convince them of sin, to bring them to the Saviour, and to enforce Christian duty in all its branches, because God's Word has an authority above every other.

The testimony of Dr. Dabney concerning the eloquent Randolph is also interesting in this connection:

> I once asked a sensible, plain man, who was familiar with the popular oratory of Randolph, what was its charm with the common people. He did not mention, as I expected he would, his magic voice, his classic grace, the purity of his English, his intense passion, the energy of his will, his pungent wit, his sarcasm, or the inimitable aptitude of his illustrations. But he answered, "It is because Mr. Randolph was so instructive; he taught the people so much which they had not known before."

The author has always felt that, unless someone in the congregation had learned something about the Bible or Christian experience which he had not known before, the sermon had done very little, if any, lasting good. The possibility of such a failure is greatly diminished, if not excluded, by expository preaching.

The Precedent

It has already been pointed out that those whom we esteem as the outstanding examples and the peers of pulpit excellence, both in Biblical and also in ecclesiastical history for sixteen centuries, at least, were almost exclusively confined to this method. It is hardly possible, or even probable, that we should excel or even compare favorably with them by use of the same method, much less by the use of some inferior method. As Dr. Pattison says:

> Revivals of religion have been marked by an increased reverence for the precise words of God, while the great masters of topical preaching have sometimes mourned that their sermons rarely led to conversions.

If it should be questioned that these truths are applicable to this present day, we would set forth this acknowledgment which appeared in a religious journal:

> After ten years of topical, textual, and general preaching, I have spent the last three years in expository preaching entirely, with these results: More souls have been saved, more improvements have been made to church properties, and more money has been given to missionary causes than in any similar period in the church's history; and it was God working through His Word that did it all!

Surely we shall not go wrong in following the precedent of those who have had such successful and fruitful ministries, by following the expository method.

The Enlargement—Personal

There is always a tendency to follow the path of least resistance, choosing that which appeals most strongly to us, and the preparation of sermons is no exception to this rule. Textual and topical preaching has a tendency to cater to this weakness.

Scholl says of exposition:

> This kind of preaching includes, naturally and without effort, a greater variety in teaching, and is thus better adapted to the various wants of souls. It is opposed to that uniformity in the choice of subjects, and the exclusive tendencies to which preachers are too much inclined.

On the other hand the expositor will be obliged to explore hitherto unknown territory and enter new paths which had previously held no appeal for him at all. His mind will be enlightened and his spirit edified, regardless of whether or not he ever makes sermonic use of his findings. His own understanding of divine revelation will be enlarged, with the result that both he and others will profit thereby. Dr. William Evans rightly remarks:

> No preacher can adopt the expository method of proclaiming truth without himself being very greatly indoctrinated and enriched by the study of the Word.

Then, too, new avenues of thought will be opened up, and before he has finished one series of messages another one, totally different, will already be formulating in his mind. Both the expositor and the congregation will come to have a better grasp of the Word as a whole, and will experience maturity together. That is one reason why the expositor never wears out. It also follows that the man who gives first place to exposition will be far more Biblical in all the rest of his preaching.

Dr. Jeff D. Ray's testimony is worthy of consideration:

> After more than fifty years of studying this preaching task, and after some thirty years of teaching the business of sermon making, I am fully convinced that expository preaching is the ideal method—that it is the method most profitable, both to the preacher and to the people. I hope no one will shy off from it when I frankly admit that it is the most difficult method.

The Enlargement—Congregational

Instead of disconnected, disjointed, fragmentary truths, seemingly unrelated the one to the other, and without unified significance, the expositor will be able to tie everything together, so that one will complement the other and be mutually enlightening to the congregation.

"No . . . scripture is of any private [separate] interpretation" but it is a part of a unified system of doctrine. So it is that the expositor will be able to develop a congregation into a body of interpreters who will learn to compare Scripture with Scripture, making their own personal discoveries to their delight and edification. Quoting again from Evans and Scholl, respectively:

> No congregation can sit long under a ministry of this kind without being deeply instructed in the Scriptures. Thus the preacher and his audience will be kept Biblical.

> It is more suited to give the knowledge of holy Scriptures, both as a whole and in its details — to inspire a taste to meditation in this divine Word, and to teach those who study it, to read it with understanding, with reflection, and always with direct and personal application.

It has already been pointed out that, as a result of Paul's having "reasoned with them out of the scriptures," the Bereans "received the word with all readiness of mind, and *searched the scriptures daily,* whether those things were so."

That being true of unbelievers, how much more likely it will be that such a yearning for truth shall be cultivated in the hearts of Christians, with a similar searching of the Scriptures for themselves!

Dr. Francis Wayland was particularly impressed with the favorable effects of exposition upon the congregation in this respect, and wrote extensively on it. We believe that a rather extended quotation will be of real value at this point.

> That minister has nobly accomplished *his* labor who has been the means of rendering his people

earnest, devout, and intelligent students of the Scriptures. . . .

Why is it that expository preaching has so entirely died out among us? [1863] When ministers had comparatively little theological education, such preaching was very common. It was entirely destitute of theological learning, but it was simple and devout, and in most cases threw some light upon the subject, and at any rate, *generally induced the hearers to examine it for themselves.* Now, when eight or ten years are spent in the study of language, and in preparation for the ministry, we very rarely hear anything of the kind. Can it be that after all this study men are unwilling to trust themselves to explain and enforce a paragraph of the Word of God? Or is it supposed that this kind of preaching is beneath the dignity of the pulpit, and is to be resigned to Sabbath schools and Bible classes? Let every minister ask himself whether he has not been deficient in this respect.

The benefits of expository preaching are manifold: In the first place the particular passage, with its connections, the scope of the thought, with the special force of its individual expressions, are laid open to the mind of the hearer. It will henceforth be a bright spot, which will shine with a clear light in all his subsequent readings. From one such passage he will derive a more distinct knowledge of duty, from another he will seek sustaining grace in affliction; and thus his Bible will be studded with gems which he probably would otherwise never have discovered. How many of our congregations have had their Bibles thus enriched by the exposition of the minister of Christ?

By thus becoming familiar with the manner in which the minister unfolds the Word of God, *the hearer learns to do it himself.* He finds that there is an important meaning in every paragraph, and he has faith to believe that he can discover that meaning if he will.

The Bible ceases to be to him a book of riddles, or of broken, disconnected sentences, but a book which he is confident God meant him to understand. He prays for the aid of the Holy Spirit . . . with the earnest desire to know the whole will of God that he may do it.

Is it not worth the effort of a lifetime to produce such an effect as this on immortal souls — souls for whom Christ died?

Compare with it the reputation for rhetorical skill, the praise of fine writing, the thanks of shallow disciples "in language soft as adulation breathes," for the intellectual treat which they have enjoyed, and how contemptible do they all appear! It is the will of God that we should "Feed the church of God, which He hath purchased with His own blood"; and does it not become us to "be about [our] Father's business"?

This recalls to mind a comment which was made by my wife, in the early years of our marriage. Becoming accustomed to having her Bible open before her when I was delivering expository messages, she said that when she came to that same chapter in her devotional reading it yielded more spiritual refreshment and blessing than other portions of the Bible.

The Diplomacy

If there is need for diplomacy in the ministry it is

certainly not out of place in the sermon. We sometimes major on majors to the exclusion of minors. Expositional preaching will help to avoid this. Those things of seemingly less importance are not utterly unimportant. The expositor will give due recognition to them in their rightful place, as he comes to them.

There are also occasions when the minister must deal with matters which are rather delicate, sometimes very personal; there again the expositor will have the advantage. For example, if some member has no missionary vision, and perhaps has raised objections because the minister has emphasized the foreign mission program of the church; to preach a topical sermon on the subject would appear as an affront, a retaliation, or a personal thrust. If, however, even soon after a personal discussion of the matter, the expositor should come, in a series of sermons on Romans, to chapter 10, it would appear perfectly natural and logical. Instead of offense and possibly hostility, there would more likely be conviction and apprehension.

Then if a divorce should occur in the church membership and, in a series of sermons on the book of Mark, the expositor comes to deal with chapter 10, there will be no apparent emphasis for the specific benefit of a single individual.

Many an embarrassing experience can be avoided, and much truth imparted to the edification of the people, by following the expositional method.

The Balance

Dr. W. Graham Scroggie affirms, "The preacher's job is *exposition,* bringing out of the Scripture what is in it; and certainly not *imposition,* putting into it what is not there." "It is much easier to pound the Bible than to expound it, but not so profitable." The expositor preaches what he finds. It is sometimes startling what he does find when he gets into the heart of a passage. It is also surprising what he does *not* find. Many times he delves into a passage with a theme in mind, only to discover that the main thrust of that particular passage is entirely different from his preconceived theme. The honest expositor will always change his theme, he will never connect that passage with something which he had previously formulated in his mind. He need not discard his theme. If it is worthwhile there will be a passage of Scripture somewhere that will be suited to it.

Dr. E. P. Barrows has written:

> The expositor's office is to ascertain and unfold the true meaning of the inspired writers, without adding to it, subtracting from it, or changing it in any way. . . . The true expositor, taking the very words of Scripture, seeks not to force upon them a meaning in harmony with his preconceived opinions, but to take from them the very ideas the writer intended to express.

Sometimes texts and statements are taken up merely to endorse a sermonic concoction which has already crystalized in the mind of the preacher before he ever got near the Bible.

I am thinking of a man who wanted to release a tirade against athletics. He already had his sermon, material aplenty and piping hot, but he needed a text (in order to be orthodox) so he turned to 2 Peter 2:13: "Spots [I think he pronounced it sports] they are and blemishes, *sporting* themselves with their own deceivings while they feast with you." Thus he "accommodated" a text to throw a blanket condemnation on all forms of sports. Doubtless there are objectionable features to many kinds of sports, and allowing for the fact that he may have had reason for his antagonism, it was still a gross misinterpretation of the Word of God.

Perhaps a proper treatment of 1 Corinthians 9:19-27 would have been beneficial, having a balancing effect upon preacher and hearer, without doing any injustice to the Scriptures. Certainly expositional preaching will go a long way toward maintaining a proper balance in all matters of interpretation.

The Steadfastness

This last virtue has always been of great importance and most desirable, but never more than today. There has never been a time when there were more religious voices in the world than today, each one, like the "barker" at a carnival, trying to outdo the other.

Expositional preaching will serve as an antidote to the poisons of doctrinal confusion and instability.

Dr. Evans reminds us that:

The word of the preacher is to make men first *see* things, then *feel* them, then *act* upon them. If the first result is not gained, the others, of course, will fail; while often, if the first is gained, the other two will go along with it.

It is most remarkable how much consideration Paul gives to the matter of instructing the younger ministers concerning the need of indoctrinating their people so as to prevent their being led astray by false teachers and doctrines. Here are some examples setting forth both the disease and the antidote.

The disease: "Some shall depart from the faith, giving heed to seducing spirits" (1 Timothy 4:1).

The antidote: "Give attendance to reading [publicly], to exhortation, to doctrine" (1 Timothy 4:13).

The disease: There are those who "strive . . . about words to no profit, but to the subverting of the hearers" (2 Timothy 2:14), they indulge in "profane and vain babblings" (verse 16) and "foolish and unlearned questions" which "do gender strifes" (verse 23), and thus they "oppose themselves" (verse 25) and fall into "the snare of the devil, who are taken captive by him at his will" (verse 26).

The antidote: "Study to show thyself approved unto God, a workman that needeth not to be ashamed, rightly dividing [apportioning] the word of truth" (2 Timothy 2:15).

The disease: "The time will come when they will not endure sound doctrine. . . . They shall turn away their ears from the truth, and shall be turned unto fables" (2 Timothy 4:3-4).

The antidote: "*Preach the word;* be instant in season, out of season; reprove, rebuke, exhort with all longsuffering and doctrine" (verse 2).

The disease: After listing a host of deficiencies the apostle ends with this indictment: "Lovers of pleasures more than lovers of God; having a form of godliness, but denying the power thereof: from such turn away. . . . But evil men and seducers shall wax worse and worse, deceiving, and being deceived" (2 Timothy 3:4-5,13).

The antidote: "All scripture is given by inspiration of God, and is profitable for doctrine, for reproof, for correction, for instruction in righteousness: that the man of God may be perfect [mature], throughly furnished unto all good works" (verses 16-17).

The disease: "There are many unruly and vain talkers and deceivers. . . . Whose mouths must be stopped, who subvert whole houses, teaching things which they ought not, for filthy lucre's sake. . . . Jewish fables, and commandments of men, that turn from the truth. . . . They profess that they know God; but in works they deny Him, being abominable, and disobedient, and unto every good work reprobate" (Titus 1:10-11,14,16).

The antidote: "Holding [forth] the faithful word as he hath been taught, that he may be able by sound doctrine both to exhort and to convince the gainsayers. . . . Wherefore rebuke them sharply, that they may be sound in the faith" (verses 9,13).

Then there are admonitions to Timothy of a personal nature which fit right into this line of thought.

Take heed unto thyself, and unto the doctrine; continue in them: for in doing this thou shalt both save thyself, and them that hear thee (1 Timothy 4:16).

Hold fast the form of sound words, which thou hast heard of me, in faith and love which is in Christ Jesus (2 Timothy 1:13).

But continue thou in the things which thou hast learned and hast been assured of, knowing of whom thou hast learned them; and that from a child thou hast known the holy scriptures, which are able to make thee wise unto salvation [daily salvation from all entanglements] through faith which is in Christ Jesus (2 Timothy 3:14-15).

A strict adherence to the Word of God will keep the minister doctrinally well-balanced and constantly in touch with God. In this way he shall be able to keep his people in line with the truth and direct their feet into the paths of righteousness. They in turn will learn to "search the scriptures" and develop a personal discernment which will enable them to see and avoid the pitfalls themselves. It is in this way that the commission of the apostle is carried out: "The things that thou hast heard of me among many witnesses, the same commit thou to faithful men, who shall be able to teach others also" (2 Timothy 2:2).

No other type of preaching is as well adapted to carry out what Paul is advocating to these young ministers as that of exposition. You will find that the false cults and spurious religions, as well as the fanaticists, will make very few inroads into the membership of that church which has been accustomed to an expositional ministry. It will be seen by this survey that the virtues of exposition are multitudinous, while the objections are hardly worthy of consideration.

PART TWO

A PLAN

FOR EXPOSITORY PREACHING

CHAPTER 4

THE EXPEDIENCY OF EXPOSITION

THE DISTINCTION

IT IS DOUBTFUL if the standard threefold classification of sermons—topical, textual, and expository—can be improved upon. Some have thought that the biographical sermon should be classed separately, but it also will fall into one of these three categories of sermons, according to the type. For instance, a biographical sermon on a character like Jabez would be classified as a textual sermon, since all that is said of him is found in 1 Chronicles 4:9-10. A biographical sermon on Naaman the leper (2 Kings 5) would fall into the expository column. Biographical sermons on characters like Moses, David, Peter, and Paul would have to be topical, if they were at all comprehensive, because material would have to be selected from so many different portions of the Bible. One might arrange a series of expository sermons on such a well-known character, but that might be rather difficult.

63

To clarify in our minds the distinction between these three types of sermons we offer some simplified examples in outline. The *topical sermon* is the development of a theme which usually covers a good deal of territory, and may involve a number of aspects of doctrinal truth. Verses or statements from any book of the Bible, spoken of as proof texts, are woven into the outline in an orderly manner, in the development of the main theme, which is suggested by the topic. Psalm 136:1-4 would serve as a foundation for a message on being thankful to God. The sermon could be arranged as follows:

RENDER THANKS UNTO GOD

1. THE PUBLIC EXPRESSION OF THANKFULNESS

Instruction and attitude. Leviticus 22:29 — "at your own will" — it must be a willing act. Psalm 50:14-15 — first "thanksgiving" and then "call upon Me" in distress. 1 Chronicles 23:30 — "every morning" and "likewise at even" — regularly. 1 Chronicles 16:1,4,8 — thankfulness is predominant in worship.

Inspiration and activity. 1 Chronicles 29:9-13 — thanksgiving because the people had discovered the blessedness of liberal giving. 2 Chronicles 29:31 — consecration and thankfulness conjoined. Yieldedness produces thankfulness. Psalm 35:18 — the public testimony of thankfulness.

2. THE PRAYERFUL EXAMPLE OF THANKFULNESS

The positive example. Daniel 6:10 — prayerful

though his life was in jeopardy. Matthew 11:25 —
Jesus was thankful in the day of His rejection. Luke
17:15-19 — at least one of the nine (a Samaritan, no
less) was thankful, and made it known.

The persuasive example. Philippians 1:3-4 —
thankfulness leads to prayer. Philippians 4:6-7 —
thankfulness leads to peace. Colossians 2:6-7 —
thankfulness coincides with growth. Colossians 4:2-
4 — thankfulness stimulates intercession for witnessing.

3. THE PERSONAL EXTENSION OF THANKFULNESS

It is inclusive. Psalm 69:30 — melodious praise in
thanksgiving. Psalm 92:1-2 — good advice. Continued thankfulness does everybody good. Psalm
95:1-2 — united thanksgiving stimulates a joyful
people. Psalm 107:1,22 — united thankfulness
magnifies God's mercy. Plus Psalm 136:1-3.

It is individual. Psalm 116:17 — sometimes there
is a price to pay in public thankfulness. Psalm
119:62 — thankfulness is always appropriate, any
hour of the day or night. Acts 27:35 — in the
presence of danger and unbelief. What a testimony!
1 Thessalonians 5:18 and Ephesians 5:20 —
thankfulness in "all things" because of Romans
8:28. Romans 1:21 — total apostasy is the outcome
of thanklessness. Jonah 2:9 — thankfulness leads to
repentance.

Another example of a topical sermon on the idea
of being sheltered under His wings might be arranged like this. It will be noticed that all but the last
reference are found in the Old Testament. This time
we give the skeleton outline, with just the reference.

UNDER HIS WINGS

1. THE RELEASE

The providential rescue—Exodus 19:4-5; Deuteronomy 32:11-13.
The plenteous reward—Ruth 2:12 in context.

2. THE REFUGE

The paternal protection—Psalm 17:8-9; Psalm 36:7.
The personal panic—Psalm 55:4-7; Psalm 57:1; Psalm 61:4.

3. THE RELATIONSHIP

The continual rejoicing—Psalm 63:7.
The constant renewal—Isaiah 40:31. Malachi 4:2—future and eternal. Matthew 23:37—take advantage of the present provision—*now*.

You will note that the theme binds one to a single idea, but there is ample material on the subject. "God's Right Hand" would be another example of a single and somewhat circumscribed theme, though there is a lot of inspiring material for that also.

In a *textual sermon* the preacher confines himself to one or two verses of Scripture, or possibly to one sentence, or even a phrase within a sentence. This brief portion of Scripture is enlarged upon and given rather exhaustive treatment. In this case no other reference is necessary, although an occasional quotation from some other portion of the Bible might lend particular emphasis to some vital truth, or provide corroboration to what is under consideration. A textual sermon on the best-known verse in the Bible could be handled this way. The topic for John 3:16 might be "Love Superlative" or simply "God Loves You." Let us take the latter.

GOD LOVES YOU

1. THE EXTENT OF HIS LOVE

The grace of God. "So"—how much? "He gave"—not a deal, a bargain, a trade, or a swap. Not a contract, requiring qualifications, but a straight-out gift.

The greatness of God. "His Son"—the dearest and most costly gift of all. A unique gift. He is the only one of His kind. He gave Himself for us. There could be no other way, or God would have utilized it.

2. THE EXCELLENCE OF HIS LOVE

Eternal doom. "Perish"—it is inevitable without intervention by God. Eternal destiny already determined without Christ. (Note verse 18.)

Eternal deliverance. "Have eternal life"—this is made available by His death. "That"—the purpose of His death. The destiny is reversed in Christ, who is "the gift of God" (Romans 6:23). Certainty in John 3:36.

3. THE EXPERIENCE OF HIS LOVE

The condition. "Believeth"—faith, acceptance, reception, commitment, grasping, laying hold, appropriation. "Trust—cling to—rely on" (Amplified Bible).

The constituents. "Whosoever"—one of the broadest and most inclusive words in human speech. No one is excluded if he believes. No one can be included if he rejects. The other references need not be used, but they fit in very well. All that the sinner needs to know about God's love is included in the text.

In distinction to the topical and textual sermon, the *expository sermon* is a treatment of a single, extended passage of Scripture; a lengthy paragraph, a chapter or more than one chapter, or even a whole book of the Bible. The preacher will be confined in his treatment to the passage in hand, but will be very unlikely to attempt an exhaustive treatment of the passage. The following is a very simple and concise outline of Acts 3:1-11. You will notice that the topic is composed of the words of Scripture itself. The major headings are confined to one word also.

LEAP, YE LAME

1. LOOKING

The place. They were in the right place, with the right objective. Prayer is vital, particularly when the testimony of the church is at stake.

The person. The cripple depicts a helpless sinner, totally dependent—"was carried"—"laid daily." He asked assistance, and received more than he expected. "Look on us"—what does the world see when it looks on us?

2. LIFTING

The resources. "In the name of Jesus Christ"—is

the secret of power to lift sinners out of despair. We have something better than "silver and gold" to offer a needy world.

The results. "The right hand"—needy people deserve the best we have to offer. We must give them a lift. Someone gave me a lift. "Immediately . . . strength"—from God Himself. Neither the cripple nor the apostles could provide that. When the man *looked* he was *lifted.*

3. LEAPING

The triumph. A Christian lifts—God strengthens—the sinner leaps. "Leaping—stood—walked—entered—walking—leaping—praising." The evidence of a real conversion. *That is living.*

The testimony. "And all the people saw him walking and praising *God*—not Peter and John. "And they knew . . . and they were filled with wonder and amazement." Public profession always has a good effect upon the community when it is genuine. "All the people ran together . . . greatly wondering." That is exactly what should happen when a man is lifted out of spiritual bondage. Let us lift someone this week, and rejoice when he leaps, and others are amazed.

Whether topical, textual, or expository, *all* preaching should be Biblical. Unfortunately this is not true of a great deal of the preaching in modern pulpits. The vast majority of sermons today could not be correctly classified in any of the three categories stated. Topical preaching is most popular, but most of it has very little Biblical content, and therefore has little authority. Textual preaching is also extant, but here also there is too little real interpretation of Bible truth. A verse of Scripture may be quoted, which suggests an idea; that idea is incorporated into a topic, and the topic is then used as a point of departure for a thirty-minute demonstration of sermonic globe-trotting. Again, a phrase or a clause is used as a topic, which is repeated half a dozen times or more during the discourse, with two or three *lengthy* anecdotes (which may not even be related) packed in between the repetitions. A minister of my acquaintance classifies this sort of thing as "bullfrog preaching — a croak and a jump."

One time I engaged a man of some repute in a conversation about preaching. I asked him what type of sermon he used most extensively, giving the familiar threefold classification. He just laughed and said he didn't know what kind he did. He said his professor advised the students to develop their own style, so he just preached; he would not know how to classify his sermons. He had sat in homiletics classes for possibly four or five years, and had been a pastor for many years, and was then quite prominent. He preached correct doctrine fervently, but it seems to me that a man with training and experience should be able to classify his sermons, even though they would not be reckoned as masterpieces in the realm of sermonic art.

Dr. Ray discerns the deficiencies and limitations of present-day preaching and analyzes it in his inimitable way:

Seventy-five years ago [over one hundred now], John A. Broadus said, "How small a proportion of the sermons heard weekly throughout the world are really good!" Although we present-day preachers have had much better opportunities, the good man's rather severe judgment applies to us even more than to the preachers of his day. Most of the men in the ministry today are good men, but most of them are not first-rate preachers. The tragedy of it is that most of them do not seem to realize that preparing and delivering sermons is the main business of the preacher. The result is that they spend more time and give more nervous energy and hard work to secondary things than they do to the major task. *They are setting hens on porcelain eggs.* (Italics ours.)

Speaking from an octogenarian standpoint Dr. Ray offers this personal testimony concerning the value of expository preaching:

I know that genuine expository preaching is almost as rare as the once multitudinous buffalo on our Texas prairies. If you ask me why, I can tell you. I found it not in a book nor by observation of other preachers. I found it out by personal, practical experience. When I am to make a sermon, I have found it an easy job, quickly performed, to deduce a topic from a text and make a rhetorical outline of that topic and dress it up in platitudinous superficialities and palm it off as a message from the Word of God. But I have found it difficult, laborious, and time-consuming to dig out an adequate interpretation of a passage of Scripture and coordinate the results of that patient digging in an effective, logical outline. Because I have allowed so

many little "higglety-pigglety," inconsequential
enterprises to break in on my time, I have felt it
necessary to follow the line of least resistance and
thus have I, and doubtless thus have you, formed
the habit of preparing mainly topical sermons. I am
an "old dog" now and they tell me that it is hard to
teach an antiquated canine a new trick, but I say to
you solemnly that if I could call back fifty years, I
should make it a life's ambition to be a real expositor of the Word rather than a rhetorical
declaimer on topics and mottoes.

His ability to discern and his own humble confession, along with a ripe and varied experience, all
lend a great deal of weight to his final prediction:

The man with a passion for exposition and a gift
for attractively and forcefully expounding the Word
of God is the coming preacher.

Dr. Faris D. Whitesell is emphatic in his affirma-
tion concerning the relative value of the expositional
method:

This is the favorite method of scriptural
preaching for most Biblical preachers. It sticks
closest to the Bible, submits more completely to the
authority of the Bible, and most highly honors the
Word of God.

Above all other methods, it takes the Bible as it is,
and seeks to find and apply the true grammatical-
historical-contextual meaning.

Expository preaching is at its best when a
preacher is expounding a book of the Bible, section
by section, in his best homiletical style. And, since
the expository preacher will wish to hold himself on
the straight track of God's revealed truth, he will

often, perhaps usually, take a longer passage than a single verse. The key idea to remember about expository preaching is that it is explanatory. Herrick Johnson says: "But explanatory discussion has its chief crown and glory in what is technically known as expository preaching. This preaching is based upon a somewhat extended section of Scripture. But while the chief business of expository preaching is explanation, it is always explanation in order to persuasion. It is not mere commentary." The ideal explanatory discussion is that which so exhibits God's truth by narration, description, exemplification, or exposition, that it not only makes the meaning absolutely clear, but also shows a distinct and dominating purpose to reach the will and move it Godward.

In going into the matter of what an expository sermon *is,* it might be well to point out what it is *not.*

It is not a running commentary. Some men "run" through a chapter or a passage of Scripture, commenting here and there upon a word, a sentence, or even a whole verse, thinking that by so doing they are preaching an expository sermon. Very often this is a subterfuge for lack of preparation. Of course there may be times when this practice could be done to good advantage, under certain circumstances. In former generations gifted men gave "Bible readings" which were well thought out and effectively executed, but that is pretty well a thing of the past, so far as this writer can tell. At any rate, that is not an expository sermon.

It is not a Bible study. There is a definite need for

a systematic, exegetical study of a book of the Bible, when theological and doctrinal truths are set forth, as in the class room (though on a congregational level) for the instruction and edification of God's people, but this is not expository preaching either.

What then is expository preaching?

Dr. G. Campbell Morgan defines preaching in general:

> Preaching is the declaration of the grace of God to human need on the authority of the Throne of God; and it demands on the part of those who hear that they show obedience to the thing declared.

Because he was an outstanding expositor, I am inclined to believe that Dr. Morgan had expository preaching in mind, at least more than any other method. when he said that.

Dr. F. B. Meyer has a much more extensive definition, which applies most directly to the expositional method:

> The consecutive treatment of some book or extended portion of Scripture on which the preacher has concentrated head and heart, brain and brawn, over which he has thought and wept and prayed, until it has yielded up its inner secret, and the spirit of it has passed into his spirit. . . . It is not an artifice or a trick; it is probably the possession of a man's nature by the Spirit which hides in true and sacred words, as sparks lie hid in flint. . . . The highest point of sermon utterance is when a preacher is "possessed," and certainly, in the judgment of the writer, such possession comes oftenest and easiest to a man who has lived, slept, walked,

and eaten in fellowship with a passage for the best part of a week.

This, of course, includes both preparation and delivery as well as the sermon itself. The product is an expository sermon.

Dr. Ray asks the question, "What is exposition?" and then gives this answer:

In preaching, exposition is the detailed interpretation, logical amplification, and practical application of a passage of Scripture.

For my own understanding I would suggest something like this:

Expository preaching is the technique of developing and presenting extended passages of Scripture in an understandable manner, applying the truth to capture the interest and secure a favorable response from the listener.

Doubtless that definition could be greatly improved upon. Definitions are of little value anyway unless they create an understanding, but I believe the reader will now have a pretty fair idea of what we have in mind when we use the term expository preaching. Dr. Whitesell aptly says:

We do not find agreement among writers on homiletics as to the nature of expository preaching. They do agree that there are some things which it is *not*. It is not merely rambling comment, nor exegesis, nor analysis, nor pure explanation. It is more than all or any of these. It utilizes all of the fundamental homiletical processes and presents a complete sermon.

Whether or not you are in full agreement with the author's conception of what expository preaching really is, we believe that you will conclude that this type of preaching is highly beneficial and most desirable in the pulpits today.

Dr. Pattison summarizes it all in one short, powerful sentence:

> When we proceed to the exposition of a complete passage of Scripture we pass to a much higher kind of preaching.

THE DIVERSITY

It has been stated previously that there are some who feel that the expository method does not allow sufficient room for variety; that there is far too much repetition, too much sameness. That is not true; in fact, the exact opposite is true. By the treatment of different books in the Bible, as well as many separate extended passages, the preacher will be constantly entering new areas and making new discoveries in fresh territory hitherto untouched. Consequently there will be far *less* likelihood of repetition.

A minister who was in the process of changing pastorates made this significant remark to a ministerial friend who had occupied another pulpit in that same city for a number of years: "I have been here for five years and it is time for me to move. I am a topical preacher, and all the best topics are exhausted in five or six years. You are an expository preacher and you can stay on here indefinitely."

Robert Murray McCheyne was noted for his expository ability. Dr. Andrew A. Bonar says of him:

It was his wish to arrive nearer the primitive mode of expounding Scripture in his sermons. Hence, when one asked him if he was never afraid of running short of sermons some day, he replied, "No; I am just an interpreter of Scripture in my sermons; and when the Bible runs dry, then I shall." And in the same spirit he carefully avoided the too common mode of accommodating texts—fastening a doctrine on the words, not drawing it from the obvious connection of the passage. He endeavored at all times to preach the mind of the Spirit in a passage; for he feared that to do otherwise would be to grieve the Spirit who had written it.

As to the reaction to his preaching, on the part of his parishioners, Mr. Bonar testifies as follows:

But on common Sabbaths (regular days of meeting) also, many soon began to journey long distances to attend St. Peter's—many from country parishes, who would return home with their hearts burning, as they talked of what they had heard that day.

There is unlimited variety and diversity for the expositor, even when he is giving a consecutive treatment of a whole book of the Bible in course. As to the matter of preaching miscellaneous chapters or passages there will easily be found several for any purpose or occasion. For instance, suppose we make a rather general classification of sermons like this: historical, biographical, revival, evangelistic, consecration, missionary, stewardship, prayer, doctrinal. Most sermons would fall into one of these groups, with the possible exception of sermons for special occasions such as Christmas, Mother's Day, Thanksgiving, and so on. Of course there is overlapping there, because a historical sermon might be any one of the others. Nevertheless, this general distinction will serve to illustrate what we have in mind concerning variety.

Historical

For rich preaching on historical passages one can immediately turn to the book of Genesis. There is plenty of this kind of material in Genesis for a series of sermons which would cover from eight to eighteen months of continuous exposition. Likewise the books of Judges, Ruth, Samuel, Kings, Chronicles, Ezra, Nehemiah, and Esther in the Old Testament lend themselves very readily to historical exposition. Then in the New Testament, the book of Acts is one of the most fertile, inspiring, delightful, and fruitful fields for a series of expository messages, which will take perhaps seven or eight months, or even more, to complete. The preacher who cannot make those historical chapters in Acts live and pulsate with spiritual life and power might well look into his own experience and condition before God. There are many historical portions to be found in other books of the Bible which are considered primarily doctrinal and ethical in their approach. It will take a very long time to exhaust the historical chapters of the Bible.

Biographical

There is also abundance of material in the realm of biographical exposition. Such Old Testament characters as Noah, Abraham, Jacob, Joseph, Moses, and David are among the first to come to mind, considering the noble and triumphant. Then, to present the other side of the picture, one might use Cain, Esau, Haman, Ahab, Jezebel, and Athaliah. Men of weak character are epitomized in Lot, Samson, Balaam, and Eli.

In the New Testament there is John the Baptist, Peter, Nicodemus, the Samaritan woman, Philip, Paul, and many others who are outstanding, each in his own right. Demas, Alexander, Diotrophes, and others represent undesirable characteristics. In some cases, such as Naaman the leper, the biography will likely be confined to one sermon on one chapter. In other cases the preacher will take just one experience in the life of a man, such as David's gracious attitude toward Mephibosheth in 2 Samuel 9, with the topic, "Lame Feet."

On the other hand it may seem propitious to preach a whole series of biographical sermons on characters like Joseph, Moses, or Paul. The author has four such sermons on Gideon, and four on Balaam.

Revival

When the matter of revival requires a concerted emphasis, one can find a good many chapters which are appropriate for that purpose. Probably one of the first to come to mind in this connection is 2 Chronicles 7. It is customary to deal with the fourteenth verse as a textual sermon, and it is ideal. However, though the fourteenth verse is the core of the chapter, the whole passage is rich with suggestive material. It is very well to show how we can *have* revival, as that one verse portrays; but these are days when we also need to emphasize what we may expect if we do *not* have revival, which will surely be the case (and is) when we fail to meet the requirements. In verses 19 and 20 God says: "But if ye turn away, and forsake My statutes and commandments . . . Then will I pluck them up by the roots. . . ."

In 2 Chronicles 34 we have the account of a "limited" revival under Josiah. It was great as far as it went, but it did not go far enough. It was limited because the people did not go all out for God.

Nehemiah 8, Isaiah 1, Psalms 51, 85, and 126 are all suggestive for revival challenges.

Evangelistic

It is doubtful if there is a book in the Bible which cannot produce a chapter or passage adaptable to an evangelistic message. When it comes to evangelism it is a question of which chapter to use when.

First of all let us note the distinction between revival and evangelism. Many seem not to see much difference, and there are those who think the two are identical. This is not the case. Revival always precedes evangelism. It may be true occasionally that an evangelistic emphasis will kindle a revival fire, but only as that fire burns in the hearts of the believers will evangelism prosper. The two are almost inseparable, but when revival breaks out in the hearts of God's people, evangelism will be the inevitable result. When cold, dead Christians are stirred up to new life, vigor, and enthusiasm for God, they will then be in condition to evangelize the lost. Revival preaching is designed to rouse the Church from her stupor and bring her back into right relationship with God, while evangelistic preaching is designed to present God's way and provision of salvation for lost sinners, that they might be born again. Billy Graham says: "Revival concerns the people of God; evangelism, the unconverted."

The evangelistic message is designed to bring about "repentance toward God, and faith toward our Lord Jesus Christ" on the part of the ungodly. In this connection we immediately think of such chapters as Genesis 3 and 4; Exodus 12 and 14; Joshua 2; 1 Kings 18; Psalm 22; Isaiah 53 and 55; Daniel 5; John 3 and 4; Luke 15; Acts 9 and 10; and a whole host of others.

Dedication

The call to personal dedication of life is something

which demands constant consideration. There are many angles to it, and many phases to be set forth, but thinking of it in a general way, and with the idea of challenging the people to yield to God on this score, we could use such passages as Exodus 32, Isaiah 6, Luke 9, 1 Corinthians 6, 2 Corinthians 6, Ephesians 6, and Romans 12. I think there is hardly a book in the Bible which will not provide a passage which will be well adapted to such a challenge.

Missionary

It has been well said that the Bible is a missionary textbook, so there will be no scarcity of material on this vital theme either. For the purpose of instruction, as well as a graphic appeal, certain chapters stand out as though designed for that purpose specifically and exclusively. I am thinking of Genesis 12, Numbers 32, Isaiah 6, the book of Jonah, Matthew 28, John 21, Acts 13, and Romans 10, which are all superb. Personal soul-winning would fall in this category also, since that is missions in detail. The many interviews of Jesus, as in the case of Nicodemus in John 3; the Samaritan woman in John 4; Philip and the eunuch, Acts 8; Peter and Cornelius, Acts 10; the conversion of Paul, Acts 9; and of the Philippian jailer, Acts 16, are all abounding with richness for such a purpose.

Stewardship

When we speak of stewardship we are inclined to

place the major emphasis upon the matter of returning to God the material things of life. In this we are not bound down to "The tithe is the Lord's," or "Bring ye all the tithes into the store house." Why not preach an expository sermon on Leviticus 27, or Malachi 3? Some other prominent chapters setting forth this particular truth are Exodus 36, Luke 16 (first part), 1 Corinthians 16, and 2 Corinthians 8—9.

From the negative standpoint such characters as Achan, Gehazi, Judas, Ananias and Sapphira; positively such people as Abraham, Jacob, Araunah, Mary, Lydia, Barnabas, and Epaphroditus are all very applicable and may be treated from the expository standpoint.

Prayer

The whole concept of prayer is unlimited, and must receive generous and constant attention. Here again we are at no loss for extended passages to use in expository messages. I think we would all agree that John 17 is a real classic in this realm. Then there is Matthew 6, and the two successive parables in Luke 18 go well together. They might be treated in one message or separately, but in succession. The prayer of Solomon, on the occasion of the dedication of the Temple (2 Chronicles 6) is a striking example among these of the Old Testament. Paul's prayer for the Christians at Ephesus (Ephesians 3:13-21), which of course includes all saints of all ages, is one of the gems of intercession in the New Testament. There is an abundance of material for expository addresses in this most vital ministry of intercession and heart communion with God.

Devotion

When it comes to devotional messages designed to comfort, strengthen, edify, and inspire the saints, I suppose we would turn, by common consent, to the Psalms. One could give a brief series of devotional messages from the Psalms annually without exhausting this grand canyon of heart-warming, spiritual treasures in five or six years. Of course some of the psalms are very difficult to treat in the expository fashion, because they do not all have a continuity of thought. There are times when the psalmist just jots down precious thoughts as they come to him, without consideration of connection. Nevertheless, there are those psalms which seem to be made to order. Take for instance that beautiful trilogy of Psalms 22 — 24; Psalm 22 pictures the "Good Shepherd" of John 10 giving His life for the sheep; Psalm 23 portrays the "Great Shepherd" of Hebrews 13, risen, ascended, and interceding for His sheep; Psalm 24 presents the "Chief Shepherd" of 1 Peter 5 coming again in glory to take His sheep home to be with Himself. Psalms 34, 37, and 121 are all outstandingly comforting and uplifting. The book of Psalms is an almost inexhaustible well of living water for devotional exposition.

Other whole books of the Bible fall in this division also. The book of Ruth (the great love story); Philippians (the book of joy); and 1 Peter (the book of suffering) are all ideal for devotional exposition. A great many single chapters such as Isaiah 35 and 40, Micah 4, John 14, 2 Corinthians 1, 1 Thessalonians 4, 2 Timothy 4, along with Revelation 21 and 22 will warm and enlarge the hearts of the saints.

Doctrinal

If it be thought that we must forsake the expository method in order to indoctrinate the Church, that too is a mistake. There will always be a chapter or a passage appropriate for every doctrine, if it is a Biblical doctrine. Many traditions and unscriptural doctrines will be ruled out in this way also. We suggest a few leading doctrines just for example.

The Incarnation—John 1; Philippians 2.

The Crucifixion—John 19; all the Gospels; Psalm 22; Isaiah 53.

The Resurrection—Luke 24; 1 Corinthians 15; Philippians 3.

Repentance—Matthew 3; Luke 13.

Regeneration—Ephesians 2.

The New Birth—John 3.

Justification—Romans 3—4.

Eternal Punishment—Mark 9; Luke 16; Revelation 20.

Baptism—Matthew 3; Romans 6.

The Lord's Supper—Matthew 26; 1 Corinthians 11.

Love—1 Corinthians 13; 1 John 4.

We have suggested only choice portions for each doctrine. Doubtless your mind has already envisioned other passages in each case which would be admirably suited to a doctrinal dissertation. The book of Romans is, of course, the cream of them all. It runs the gamut of Christian doctrine from first to last and never fails to thrill the hearts of God's people, as well as to instruct the sinner, when covered consecutively in a series of expositions.

It is doubtful if there could ever arise a situation or an occasion when the preacher would necessarily have to forsake the expository method in order to meet it, and do it naturally and adroitly.

If you are launching a building program, 2 Kings 6:1-7 and both chapters of Haggai are superb. The whole book of Nehemiah is also excellent for a series at such a time.

The commencement sermon—Psalm 1; 1 Kings 18; Daniel 1 and 6; 2 Timothy 4.

An ordination sermon—Jeremiah 1; Ezekiel 2 and 3 (together); Daniel 1; John 15.

Funerals—Many Psalms, such as 116; John 11 and 14: 1 Corinthians 15: 1 Thessalonians 4.

Christmas—Luke 1 and 2; Matthew 1 and 2: Isaiah 7.

Mother's Day—2 Chronicles 22 (a wicked mother): Genesis 27 (an indulgent mother): 1

Samuel 1 (a triumphant mother); 2 Timothy 1 (an ideal mother).

Thanksgiving—Many of the Psalms; Matthew 11; Luke 17.

Obviously this is not intended to be exhaustive but suggestive. It is sufficient to indicate that one need never forsake the expository method for lack of an extended passage to fit properly the need or occasion. There will be times when a topical or textual sermon will be both desirable and essential, but not due to the fact that there is nothing available in the expositional realm.

Exposition is adapted to all ages. Young people and children will be alert to grasp Bible truth if it is presented in an understandable manner. Mr. Herder says:

> In my view the exposition of Scripture is the highest and best kind of preaching, especially in our times; and in particular, I regard it as the best and safest mode for young persons.

A contemporary pastor wrote the author in this connection: "I give expositions of Bible books morning and evening to my congregation. I find it feeds the flock, *grips young people,* sustains interest."

I recall two experiences along this line. One Sunday morning I remarked to my wife that this was one time that I would be preaching over the heads of the young people, but I felt it was necessary. I was attempting to treat 1 John 4, taking as a subject, "The Analysis of Love." After the service an eleven-year-old girl, who had listened intently, said, "Mother, that is the sweetest message the pastor has brought since he has been here." Is it necessary for me to say that those were sweet words in the pastor's ear?

Another time we were using the book of Amos. We had taken too much material, but it had captivated the pastor's heart and he just *couldn't* stop. He did not have his watch on the pulpit either (a practice which he has cultivated since). It was embarrassing to discover that the sermon lasted fifty-five minutes. Nevertheless, that patient congregation was not restless and did not yawn. It was a real shock when a mother quoted her thirteen-year-old son as saying, "It would have been all right with me if he had gone on for another hour."

Allow me to say that I do not impose on my congregations like that any more. The only reason I was excused then was because it was expository.

Dr. Jones paraphrases: "And now abideth topical, textual, and expository sermons, these three; but the greatest of these is expository."

CHAPTER 5

THE TECHNIQUE OF EXPOSITION

THE PASTORAL PREPARATION

IN CONSIDERATION of the matter of preparation it is well to keep in mind that it is a twofold process. First, there must be the preparation of the messenger and then the message, and they must always be in that order. The usefulness of the latter will depend entirely upon the completeness of the former. Let the messenger be prepared of the Lord and then God will enable the messenger to prepare a message for the people. Dr. Griffith Thomas has well said:

> The call of the present time on theological students, and on the younger clergy in particular, is to give special attention to preaching. Both in theological colleges and in parochial work, we must make preparation for preaching a prominent feature and factor of our clerical life. We must give the best we can in matter and manner. We must work as hard as we can in order to produce the best results. No time, no strength, no thought, no effort,

can be too much to devote to this duty. Even if this means the surrender of parochial organizations, the result in the long run will not be harmful, but advantageous. It may be that *we need to do less in order to do more.*

The unlearned (who often prefer to remain in that category) frequently take the position that training and preparation are not necessary. They feel that all they need to do is to open the yawning cavity which leads to the esophagus and a great stream of sermonic utterance will automatically emerge. Such men are inclined to glory in their ignorance, justify laziness, and are usually very critical of any man who seeks to have his ministry enhanced by making adequate preparation. They are constantly misinterpreting and abusing Psalm 81:10, the last part of which reads: "Open thy mouth wide, and I will fill it." Taken in its context, with nothing more than the first part of the verse, which reads, "I am the LORD thy God, which brought thee out of the land of Egypt," it obviously means that the wonder-working God who wrought such a marvelous deliverance from Egypt is still abundantly able to provide for His children. When His people will wait before Him, as the little bird in the nest awaits the worm, with wide-open mouth, they may rest assured that He will fill it with the nutritions of divine truth, hence *they* shall be filled. When the minister has so waited upon the Lord for such fullness, he then masticates and digests the Spirit-revealed truth and prepares to give it to others in a manner that will be conducive to their reception. The minister is under such a holy and imperative obligation and, under the guidance of God, must ever seek to present this truth with clarity and emphasis, in a systematic and thorough manner. This can be accomplished only with careful and studious preparation.

In this matter of sermon preparation there is no substitute for work—spade work—hard work—laborious *work*. This is even more true of exposition than of any other method. Let those who seek to excel in the realm of exposition recognize to begin with that there is no shortcut or easy road to success. It is easier to "get by" with any other type of sermon, if there is a tendency to avoid hard work. Dr. W. B. Riley was well qualified to speak with authority on this matter, and he said:

> It is my candid judgment that the average sermon has cost the preacher entirely too little mental endeavor. Among the reasons that there are not more great preachers is the fact that there are so few painstaking students. Good preaching is only and ever the product of great study.

Charles Haddon Spurgeon also had a word to say in this connection:

> Your pulpit preparations are your first business, and if you neglect these, you will bring no credit upon yourself or your office. Bees are making honey from morning till night, and we should be always gathering stores for our people. I have no belief in that ministry which ignores laborious preparation.

Let us give heed to the words of Solomon, that

sagacious and eloquent "preacher" of the Old Testament:

> My son, if thou wilt receive my words, and hide my commandments with thee; So that thou incline thine ear unto wisdom, and apply thine heart to understanding; Yea, if thou criest after knowledge, and liftest up thy voice for understanding; If thou seekest her as silver, and searchest for her as for hid treasures; Then shalt thou understand the fear of the LORD, and find the knowledge of God (Proverbs 2:1-5).

As the prospector pursues his precipitous course in search of the precious ore, and the diver scours the ocean floor in search of treasure, so must the minister delve into the Scriptures for that knowledge which edifies and enriches.

"Blessed [happy] is the man . . . [whose] delight is in the law of the LORD; and in His law doth he meditate day and night" (Psalm 1:1-2).

"This book of the law shall not depart out of thy mouth; but thou shalt meditate therein day and night, that thou mayest observe to do according to all that is written therein: for then thou shalt make thy way prosperous, and then thou shalt have good success" (Joshua 1:8).

Such excellent advice is probably more applicable to the minister than to anyone else and, if followed sincerely and conscientiously, carries with it the promise of real success. It works most admirably in the realm of exposition.

"If any of you lack wisdom, let him ask of God,

that giveth to all men liberally, and upbraideth not; and it shall be given him" (James 1:5).

That minister who will take time to call upon God expectantly, and will faithfully await His response, will not be disappointed.

"Thy words were found, and I did eat them; and Thy word was unto me the joy and rejoicing of mine heart" (Jeremiah 15:16).

The timid, retiring, and persecuted prophet found his own heart stirred when God's Word was absorbed into his very being. He was so thrilled that his depression was turned into rejoicing.

"Then I said, I will not make mention of Him, nor speak any more in His name. But His word was in mine heart as a burning fire shut up in my bones, and I was weary with forbearing, and I could not stay" (Jeremiah 20:9). Again, under stress and strain of persecution, with his life in jeopardy, he determined that he would preach no more. Nevertheless, by virtue of the fact that he was literally saturated with the Word, it was like a consuming fire that simply had to find release. He could not contain himself. It was not the result of a sudden inspiration, or an overnight exhilaration, but the outcome of a constant and continual poring over divine truth until it had taken possession of him.

It is only after hours of concentrated perusal of the Word that you are overcome by a holy enthusiasm, and are then in a position to impart it to others in such a way as to create within them a similar longing and desire for living truth. The Bereans "searched the scriptures daily" to examine what was actually there. That is the main business and objective of the minister. Having found what is there we are under obligation to impart it as it is, in its purity, in its unity, in its entirety, with simplicity of understanding. Jesus counseled us to "Search the scriptures; for . . . they are they which testify of Me" (John 5:39).

All of this takes time, a great deal of time. Our homiletics professor advised us never to undertake to preach a new sermon (one which had not been previously prepared and used) until we had spent at least six hours in preparation. That is a very conservative limitation, particularly in the realm of exposition. When preparing his analysis of the books of the Bible, Dr. G. Campbell Morgan read a book through *fifty* times consecutively before putting pen to paper. His volumes of pure, chapter-by-chapter exposition (of which, in our opinion, there are none better) give evidence of long hours of diligent toil, concentrated meditation, grueling research, and mental alacrity. He said that he always gave the morning hours to this work, never reading a newspaper until after one o'clock. It paid great dividends.

A seminary professor was endowed with a fertile imagination. A student once approached him and elaborated most extravagantly upon this talent, stating that he felt that he would be a success also, if only he had an imagination comparable to that of the professor. When he had thoroughly exhausted himself, the professor replied, "Son, it's about five per cent imagination, and ninety-five per cent perspiration." So it is. W. J. Dawson once said, "Half the bad theology in the world is due to suppressed perspiration." Mr. Spurgeon correctly remarks:

> Estimated by their solid contents rather than their superficial area, many sermons are very poor specimens of godly discourse. . . . Verbiage is too often the fig leaf which does duty as a covering for theological ignorance.

A minister once left his notes, quite inadvertently, on the pulpit, and was about to leave the church. A young man, noticing the oversight, brought the notes to him. As he glanced at the paper he detected some smudges on the closely written sheet. Upon questioning the minister as to the source of the blots, he received the terse reply, "Sweat and tears." They are inseparable and essential. Someone has rightly advised: "Prepare your message as though everything depended upon yourself. Then set it aside and pray as though everything depended upon God." That is excellent advice. God does not, cannot, will not, and never has blessed laziness. He will undertake in a very real way in a providential emergency, but presumption will result in embarrassment and failure.

It seems fitting that we introduce, at this juncture, an extended quotation from Dr. Broadus:

> We turn now to the case of continuous exposition. Here, as has been intimated, the first thing to be done is to make a careful study beforehand of the entire book, or other portion of Scripture to which

the series is to be devoted. To view every book as a whole, to grasp its entire contents, and then trace in detail the progress of its narrative or argument, is a method of Scripture study far too little practiced. One of the benefits of expository preaching is that it compels the preacher to study in this way. We may say, in general, that no man will succeed in expository preaching unless he delights in exegetical study of the Bible, unless he loves to search out the exact meaning of its sentences, phrases, words. In order to do this, a knowledge of the original languages of Scripture is of course exceedingly desirable, but it is by no means indispensable. Andrew Fuller, who dealt largely and successfully in this method of preaching, had substantially no knowledge of Hebrew and Greek, and his writings were devoted not to commentary, but to didactic and polemic theology. Yet he loved to study the very words of Scripture. In all his works it is manifest that he did not content himself with gathering the general meaning of a passage, but was exceedingly anxious to know its exact meaning.

One of the most eloquent Baptist ministers of America, in the earlier part of this century, was never so happy, so charming, as in expository sermons. He, too, was unacquainted with Greek and Hebrew, and was not liberally supplied with commentaries; but he loved, above all things, to ponder and to talk about the meaning of God's Word. [The author here alludes to his kinsman, the celebrated Andrew Broadus, Sr., of Caroline County, Virginia, who, though a man of remarkable gifts and much sought after, preferred, all his life, a country pastorate. — D.]

There appears to have been a change in this respect which is to be lamented. We have a great multiplication of commentaries, and an immense amount of more or less real study of the Scriptures in the Sunday schools; we have many more ministers than formerly who know something of the original languages; but there is reason to fear that the close, thoughtful, lovingly patient study of the Bible is less common among the ministry now than it once was. As to conversation about the meaning of this or that passage, such as once abounded when preachers were thrown together, it has gone out of fashion. A man who should raise such a question now among a group of ministers, sojourning together during the session of some association or convention, would be almost stared at.

THE PROJECTIONAL PREPARATION

We come now to consider the preparation of *the message itself*. I suppose that the classic expression of all time relative to this vital matter of preparation is found in the homiletic treatment by Griffith Thomas: "We must think ourselves empty: read ourselves full: write ourselves clear: and pray ourselves keen." That is indeed a concise, but complete schedule, and we should consider each phrase separately and minutely.

"We must think ourselves empty." That certainly comes first. We cannot do much original thinking if our minds are taken up with ideas and thoughts from other sources. Let our own mental resources be exhausted before turning to other sources. (I have found that this usually does not consume too much valuable time.) It pays to stay with the text until you

have squeezed from it the very last drop of juice that you possibly can, before turning to any other library of information. Of course that does not exclude the various versions and translations, or lexicons. By the time that you have fully exhausted your own personal store of original thinking you will have a fairly good foundation for your message. In speaking of his own procedure Dr. Morgan said:

> For years I have made it a very careful and studied rule never to look at a commentary on a text, until I have spent time on the text alone. Get down and sweat over the text yourself. That is my method. . . . The text is the sermon, and to that the preacher gives himself in serious thought. It may be that is one of the most difficult things to do, but the habit once acquired, becomes one of the joys of life — real, personal, unbiased thinking. It is so easy, especially when one has built up a library, to look at the text, and then turn around and put the hand on a book. It is a real peril. There must be firsthand thinking, actual work, critical work on the text.

"Read ourselves full." Having completed your own original explorations in the text you will turn to the commentaries, expositions, word studies, and sermons by the leading scholars of the centuries. In many cases you will find that you have already drawn from the text a great deal of that which others have had revealed to them. In some cases you will seem to have unearthed rich nuggets of truth which have apparently been undiscovered by others. This will encourage you to be more diligent than ever in seeking first for original findings.

On the other hand, you will also find that you have been on the wrong track in some cases, and have passed over some very significant truths which will add a richness to your message. Many errors can be avoided this way, and much useful material will be gathered along the way, for present as well as for later use. Finally, you will cull out what appears to be extraneous or inappropriate for this particular occasion, and use that which is fitting and applicable.

"Write ourselves clear." I am sure that most of us have fallen short at this point. I suspect that very few ministers write out in full both sermons each week. However, though we may not make a practice of doing that; or even if we never make a practice of writing out a sermon in full; it is well to constantly write out sentences and paragraphs. It will train our minds to think systematically, clearly; it will develop our vocabulary; it will cultivate clarity of speech and fullness of expression, as well as simplicity of explanation. The more we write the better we shall speak, though we may not say a great deal that we put on paper. It is almost as necessary to say the thing in the right way as to say the right thing. Writing will go a long way toward efficiency in this respect. Sometimes it will be well worth while to write out sermons after they have been preached, even though you have no aspirations in the realm of publication. The author has written a lot of things which have not been published. It may be just as well that some of them were not.

"Pray ourselves keen." This is rightly stated last, but not because it is least. While there will be prayerful attitude all the way through, that the Spirit of God shall overshadow all of our preparatory activities, there must be that final turning of the whole thing over to God. Mind and heart must always be coordinated. When we feel that we have a firsthand grasp of the truth contained in the passage under consideration, we need to get on our knees and ask God to put fire into the facts. The slogan of one Christian institution is "Knowledge on Fire." We must pray that God will make the truth which He has revealed to our minds a living thing in our hearts, and a reality in our own experience, for only then can we hope to preach convincingly and powerfully. To carry on traffic in unfelt truth is a dangerous and unprofitable undertaking.

Having done all in our power to make adequate preparation of both the messenger and the message, we turn directly to God and ask Him to prepare the hearts of those who shall hear it; and to help us to deliver it in such a way as to enable the Holy Spirit to bring about results, which will obviously serve to glorify God in the lives of all concerned.

The combination of these four distinctive and guiding principles will assure the kind of success which God desires for us, and guarantee satisfactory results. The minister who is diligent in these matters, faithfully committing all into the hands of God for His approval, endorsement, and endowment of divine grace to present the finished product to the people as He shall direct, will be able to testify with the psalmist: "My heart was hot within me, while I was musing the fire burned: then spake I with my tongue" (Psalm 39:3).

THE PRESENTATION

Analysis, exegesis, interpretation, and illustration are all combined in expositional preaching. A correct analysis of the content of the passage, setting forth the main theme in orderly and systematic fashion, is most helpful to both the preacher and the audience. The message will be more efficiently delivered, and more easily understood and remembered if it is properly analyzed. The detailed unfolding of certain statements and expressions in the passage will be essential to a proper understanding of the whole. Likewise, the summarizing of certain doctrinal tenets of the faith will also be vital to the objective of the message. Difficult and major points need to be illustrated simply, in order to make the discourse understandable to all present. The presentation of the whole is your exposition.

In the realm of art the mallet, the chisel, the pounding, the chipping, the smoothing, the polishing, the arranging of the pedestal, must all be completed before the sculpture is ready to be unveiled. The mortar and pestle, the meticulous measuring and weighing of ingredients must all take place before the chemist can compound the health-producing medicament. Likewise, in the realm of exposition there must be the combining of knowledge and technique to produce the life-giving message of truth by the Holy Spirit, through mortal mind and lips.

The exposition may be a comparatively short paragraph, or just a segment of a lengthy narrative; it may be the complete section; it may include the entire chapter, involving more than one complete unit; or it may be a whole book of the Bible, as the occasion seems to demand.

For instance, one might take the entire thirty-six verses of the third chapter of John, dealing with the new birth in a very comprehensive manner. Following the discourse of Jesus with Nicodemus (verses 1-21) is the testimony of John the Baptist (verses 22-30) and finally the testimony of the author of the fourth Gospel himself (verses 31-36). Each section enforces, emphasizes, and enlarges upon the testimony of Jesus Himself relative to the new birth.

If one were to treat the narrative biographically, dealing with Nicodemus as a character, then verses 1-21 would be a complete text. (Allusion might be made to John 7:50-52 and John 19:38-39, but not necessarily so.)

Verses 14-18 comprise a paragraph which is complete in itself for a separate discourse along the line of "Life Eternal" or some such theme, without any reference to Nicodemus as a character (though the interview would have to be mentioned) or the new birth as a distinct doctrine.

In the fourth chapter of John, you might arrange

a message on "The Outcast," or "A Woman of Samaria," or some such topic, covering verses 1-43 biographically, as a complete unit. In doing so it would probably be best to omit the paragraph covering verses 31-48. That paragraph could be treated at a different time as a missionary sermon, or some phase of soul-winning, or perhaps at Thanksgiving season, since that is the harvest time.

In treating a chapter like 1 Corinthians 13, there is almost the necessity of covering it in its entirety. To do otherwise would seem to mutilate it. It is a gem of such perfection that it defies dissection, and demands a platinum setting all its own. In fact, one hesitates to expound it at all, lest it should become soiled in our unworthy hands. There seems to be an apology due before attempting it, and a feeling of inadequacy when it is over. If ever a preacher addresses a congregation disadvantageously it is at such a time. Let us beware lest we "butcher" such spiritual masterpieces.

Now let us give attention to some *guides* to the preparation of expository discourses. As has already been stated, the ideal pulpit ministry is the consecutive exposition of a book of the Bible, chapter by chapter (or section by section) Sunday after Sunday. In the first place, the people will know what is in store for them the next Lord's day, and many of them will read ahead, and be somewhat prepared at least for the message.

The preacher does not have to be casting about in his mind, trying to reach a conclusion as to what he should preach next. It is not a question of simply finding something to preach, but *which one* shall I preach? Only those who are in the ministry can fully appreciate the difficulty of reaching a decision regarding the next sermon. This difficulty is eliminated by following the consecutive procedure. Then, if occasion demands, and the Spirit of the Lord makes it apparent that something else is imperative, one can turn aside for a Sunday and resume the series the following week. That will do no injury if it happens just occasionally, which is probable.

Of course, one cannot always follow the consecutive plan fifty-two Sundays in the year; we doubt the wisdom of doing so, unless specifically led of the Lord in that way. Nevertheless, it is well to do so frequently, and as often as possible. The more you do it the greater will be the demand for it. The people will come to love it and want it always. However, regardless of the procedure followed, the Lord will have some means by which He will guide His servant to the right Scripture at the right time. Much helpful advice is given, on the matter of the selection of a text, in some of the volumes of general homiletics.

When treating a book of the Bible consecutively, it is well to read the whole book through consecutively to begin with. If it is a very long book read at least the first main section of it carefully, to get a bird's-eye view of the whole. Then read through meditatively the first chapter or section which you are going to expound, in its entirety, in order to get a grasp of the whole content, at least in a general sense, also to notice the most obvious divisions. Then go back and proceed slowly, verse by verse, sentence by sentence, word by word; "line upon line; here a little, and there a little." As the light begins to gleam through an opening here and there, jot down brief notes and possible applications. Other statements may come to mind occasionally, from other places in the Bible, so you will make comparisons and possibly put down some references, to enforce a particular point of interest or importance. Another Scripture reference may help to illustrate or unravel the truth at hand. As a rule, it is best to stick to the passage and preach the other one some other time.

Having worked your way through that passage in the Authorized Version, which is good policy because you will use it in the pulpit (if you wish to cultivate the practice of bringing Bibles to the worship service on the part of your people), you will then turn to other versions and translations. Doubtless some phrases or statements did not yield much fruit from the first gathering. It may be that things discovered toward the end of the passage will throw some new light on earlier statements, as you go back for the second reading in another version. Also, different renderings and root meanings of certain words; or a more accurate selection of words and tenses derived from other sources; or a firsthand study of the Hebrew or Greek; all will have a tendency to open up new avenues of thought and bring to the surface truths hitherto unseen. "The entrance of

Thy words giveth light; it giveth understanding unto the simple" (Psalm 119:130) is very true in the matter of sermon preparation. Continued study of the text itself will constantly yield more light upon all matters of divine revelation.

Eventually you will process the chapter with a view to analysis particularly. By this time you are familiar with the content, and are ready to formulate a topic in keeping with the theme of the passage. The logical divisions will be noted and arranged with appropriate headings. Sometimes this seems to fall together almost automatically, but there are times when it takes extended and arduous thinking to get your material systematically arranged. All of this may result in new findings in the matter of interpretation, in a doctrinal and practical unfolding of the truth. It may be that the analysis will remain incomplete until you have done practically all the research in realms apart from the Bible itself. However, it is best to get the analysis first.

Having exhausted all other sources of information you are ready for the commentaries and expositions of the scholars. How it delights the heart, and how glad you are that you exhausted your own thinking first, when you discover that the Spirit of God has unveiled to you a great deal of that which you find in the writings of others! Nevertheless, there will always be matters which were more or less enigmatical to you, or which you have overlooked, that have been made clear to others. We all have a tendency to study from that viewpoint which especially appeals to us (our "bent") or as someone has said, "our own peculiar style of awkwardness." For that reason we all make original discoveries and profit by the discoveries of others. When all of these rays of light, which have been seen by the eye of a God-given emphasis, are put into the spectrum of divine illumination, we shall have a panorama of the entire territory.

Then there must follow the deletion and elimination of all material which is extraneous to, or out of line with, the theme for this occasion, even though it be rich and desirable. It will keep, and will be of inestimable value at another time, in connection with another theme, for another occasion. It should be filed away for future reference. Many a good sermon will be salted away for future use, as a result of this research, and will thereby become a most valuable by-product of the original, later becoming its own original.

During this process it is very likely that some illustrations will have come to mind, either Biblical or otherwise, or have been found in the writings of others. Certain matters which seem to require simplifying, by use of illustration, will send you in search of an everyday occurrence, or a poem, or perhaps a verse of a hymn.

There are dangers to be avoided. There is a tendency, especially in the early days of pulpit ministry, to want to preach everything at once. We become enamored with these new revelations (rightly so) and want to pass on all of them immediately, that others may share in the blessing. You can defeat your purpose by giving too much at once. There is such a thing as spiritual dyspepsia. There have been times when I have failed to enjoy a good meal simply because the host overdid it. There was just too much good, rich food on the table at one time. A minister can make the same mistake. Too much new, rich truth at one time can create bewilderment. It is better to confine yourself at the beginning to that which will unfold the particular truth which you feel needs the emphasis. If you are uncertain about something, *leave it severely alone.* It is better to ignore it than to hash it up and be embarrassed later, when you find how badly you have blundered.

Beware of too much illustration. That is one of the greatest weaknesses of all present-day preaching, and needs to be carefully avoided in the realm of expositional preaching. The very nature of the expository method precludes the abundant use of illustrations or quotations. You have your material before you, and only where explanations are difficult do you need illustrations. Use them sparingly, and sometimes not at all.

If that truth has gripped your own heart, you will be able to impart it so that it will do the same for the people. In biographical or narrative exposition there is little need for illustrative material. Doctrinal and devotional sermons will require more in the nature of illustration.

Dr. James Black has some very practical advice to offer in connection with the use of illustrations:

Hence an illustration that does not illustrate is worse than useless—it is irritating. The true purpose of illustrating is to show the thought or idea *in action*. If it does not do that finely, you are better without it. See therefore that your illustrations are never tawdry or cheap. They may be about common things—the best always are—but they need not be commonplace. In using your illustration please do not prolong the agony! Avoid all useless or irrelevant details.

Some of us are inclined to despise illustration. Perhaps we have good reason. May Providence save us from the preacher whose sermon . . . is a string of anecdotes. I have one ministerial friend, otherwise harmless, who is afflicted with this disease. The last time I saw him he said to me, "I've got three dandy illustrations, and I am looking for a good text." That, of course, is the last ditch. Many of us would like to die *before* we reach it.

THE PROCEDURE

It is time now to formulate the outline. It is of far greater importance than some preachers think it is. Of course a man with a very analytical mind might think he had a sermon when he had nothing *but* an outline, but more often it is the other way. A man may have a lot of good material and not have it properly organized. Consequently, his presentation is poor. Truth systematically presented will always be far more effective than truth heterogeneously presented.

First of all, remember that the outline must *always*

be deduced from the passage in hand, never the converse. Never arrange an outline and then endeavor to make the passage fit the outline. The outline is not an objective in itself, but is just an aid to the objective, which is to present the teaching of the passage in relation to the subject. It is better to have a poor outline which is strictly in line with the text, than to have an artistic outline which necessitates a distortion of the text or a disproportion of truth.

An outline is not just a survey. Sometimes a man will go through a passage and jot down some ideas, thinking that he then has an outline. All he has is some suggestive material, which should then be outlined and arranged in an orderly fashion for presentation.

There are a few principles which will assist in the matter of outlining or analysis. First of all, decide on a topic. You may change the wording of it more than once before you have just what you want, but you should at least have the substance of your topic before arranging your outline. The topic, which of course incorporates your theme, must come first. Even though you are not entirely satisfied with the wording, put down something that will summarize the main line of truth which you are going to develop. The selection of the topic will be determined by the central theme of the entire passage. You need to be careful not to select a topic which includes only a portion of the passage, or a part of your message. It must be completely inclusive, and the shorter the better. Suppose you were to decide to preach an expository sermon on the conversion experience of Zacchaeus, which is related in Luke 19:1-10. Topics such as "Up a tree," "Out on a limb," "Trying to see," or "Hindrances" would certainly arouse curiosity, which is desirable, but they would have reference to only a portion of the account. Those would be good topics for a textual sermon, but not for an expository sermon, embracing the entire passage.

Such topics as "Determination," "Undaunted Initiative," "From Failure to Fruition," or "From Tree to Family" would be eye-catchers, but would also be comprehensive in their coverage.

When you have your topic, at least in substance, you will work out your divisions. The passage will always have a natural division, which will depend, to a large extent, upon the theme or particular emphasis which you have in mind at that time. The same chapter might be treated at different times, once as a biographical and later on as a doctrinal sermon. In each case the topics and the divisions would be quite different. Sometimes you will have possibly eight or ten verses in one division, and only one or two verses in another, depending upon the importance of the content or the continuity of thought therein.

There can be no hard and fast rule advanced which would apply to all sermons in connection with the number of divisions or subdivisions. I believe it is generally conceded that main divisions should be from two to five. If you go beyond five, there is a danger of becoming tedious or wearisome, and there is probably a lack of unity. Solomon said, "A threefold cord is not quickly broken." Through personal experience and the study of written sermons I have concluded that the ideal arrangement for a sermon outline is one with three major divisions and two subdivisions under each main division. There will always be exceptions to that but, for the most part, we believe that arrangement will be most beneficial to both preacher and hearer. Each main division will be a further unfolding of the main theme, as stated in the topic, and each subdivision will be a further unfolding of the truth stated in the heading of that particular division.

Continuity is the primary advantage of the outline, so be careful to *make every point line up with your subject,* which is set forth in your topic. This cannot be emphasized too much, because the whole value of your outline depends upon it. Unless every part of your outline will dovetail together with every other part, and mesh like the gears in the transmission of a car, there will be confusion, a lack of progress, and the probability of a crash.

Originality is also most desirable and highly beneficial. *Compose your own outline,* do not borrow it. You may be able to find a much nicer-looking outline in the *Pulpit Commentary* or a volume of sermons, but your own will be much more effective, simply because it is your own composition, and you know that it will work. There are several reasons for that. First of all, having created it you have a reason for every part of it; it has a vital connection with the text. Every heading is meaningful because it is the product of the passage itself. There is such a definite and vital connection between the heading and the text that a single glance is sufficient to refresh your mind concerning a whole segment of divine truth. It can readily be seen by this that, in order to originate a good outline, you must necessarily be thoroughly familiar with the passage in hand, and that requires thorough study and research. It works to advantage both ways.

A good outline will keep the preacher from wandering and also enable the listeners to retain the message a great deal longer. In this connection, it should be stated that alliteration can be most helpful. Words beginning with the same letter or having a similar sound, whether there be contrasts or comparisons expressed, will flow smoothly and have a tendency to fasten the spoken facts in the minds of the listeners. Of course this can be carried to extremes. Once someone related to me an outline on the prodigal son: it went about like this, as I recall:

THE PRODIGAL SON

1. His madness
   a. He wanted his tin
   b. He surrendered to sin
   c. He gave up his kin

2. His badness
   a. He went to the dogs

    b. He ate with the hogs
    c. He hocked all his togs

3. His gladness
    a. He was given the seal
    b. He ate up the veal
    c. He danced a reel

Some might even dare to preach a thing like that, but the man who has the audacity to do so should be asked to surrender his credentials.

The outline is to the sermon what the skeleton is to the body, so let us ever keep in mind that the pulpit is not a museum but an art gallery. The outline must be clothed with the message. To remember an outline is of little value, but to recollect a message by virtue of a well-planned outline is of inestimable and eternal value.

Having formulated an outline in keeping with your topic, and having then arranged your material under the various headings, consideration should be given to the manner in which you will present it.

First, your *introduction*. It should be well thought out and definitely planned, but brief. A wearisome introduction can ruin an otherwise good message. The connection with the context should be made clear, sometimes including what is to come, perhaps in a later message, as well as what has gone before, in order to give the true setting. Every "therefore" and "wherefore" involves at least a word of explanation concerning what has been said or written previously. Dr. B. H. Carroll has textual preaching

in mind, but his advice is excellent in the expositional realm also, when he says:

> Whenever you take a text there is always a better
> sermon in it, according to its true meaning, than
> any sermon you can preach away from it. Every
> preacher is under obligation when he selects a text
> to give its primary meaning and then its contextual
> meaning. Then he may deduce from the principles
> involved a new line of thought. But his new theme
> must be a logical development from the primary
> and contextual meaning. He should never take a
> text and preach a sermon without telling what it
> means primarily and in its context.

The introduction, showing the contextual connection, should be particularly brief in consecutive exposition, where the series is being developed with a
continuity of thought under a particular theme.
Nevertheless, the situation, the locality, the circumstances or conditions prevailing at the time; all
of these should be pointed out clearly, if the passage
requires it, before launching into the main discussion. Even in your introduction it is well to direct the
thinking of your congregation toward the main idea
that you intend to put across, so that thought will be
predominant in their minds throughout the entire
discourse.

With the core of the main theme implanted in the
minds of the people, in its true connection, you are
ready to proceed with the discussion. Blending it all
together as one complete unit you will move
smoothly and organically from one division to

another, as from movement to movement in a piece of music, building up to a grand finale and climax. Preach what you know and what inspires your own heart, and leave the rest. Give prominence to that which is vital, and do not become bogged down with needless details; there is a real danger of becoming snagged on some matter of lesser importance, thus wasting precious time that should be utilized in presenting truth which will activate your audience in heart and life. Incorporate nothing which has no direct bearing upon your main theme.

Never avoid those matters which may seem to be objectionable to some, or which present difficulties, but preach what is there without fear or favor. It is the Word of God and needs no apology. Preach "the truth, the whole truth, and nothing but the truth" as it is set forth in your text. Carry your listeners along with you, passing quickly from one level to another, ever upward, until you have them waiting with bated breath for the final climax.

Then bring the message to a definite *conclusion.* That is just as important, perhaps even more so, than the introduction. Have a properly planned stopping place. Know just how, when, and where you are going to stop, and then—*stop!* There may be no Biblical basis for it but, "Blessed is that preacher that knoweth when he is through, and then stops" is an excellent homiletical beatitude. So many otherwise good messages have been ruined because the preacher either did not know when to stop, or ignored the stop sign. One professor gave his students three good principles by which to govern their delivery: 1. Stand up. 2. Speak up. 3. Shut up.

Be sure to plan your conclusion and stick to it. When you get so enthusiastic that you feel you cannot stop, remember that the people may be feeling that they cannot sit. The whole value of your message could be ruined by prolonging your conclusion. No one has ever been offended, no one has ever become dilatory about church attendance, no one has ever become inattentive, because the sermon was *too short.* We are certainly not arguing in favor of sermonettes or devotional "talks." That sort of thing accomplishes very little in the pulpit that is of vital and lasting value. Nevertheless, you must be most careful not to impose on the most patient and appreciative people in the world — your congregation.

On the other hand, the congregation is more likely to stay with the preacher for an extended period of time, if he is delivering a well-prepared expository sermon, than otherwise.

Then, too, be sure that your conclusion really concludes the message, don't just dribble off. Bring the message to an end in such a manner that the people feel that nothing more *needs* to be said. This is *it,* now all that remains to be done is to put into practice what has been taught.

In connection with your conclusion is your final *application.* This, too, should be well planned and should blend into your conclusion. In one sense it is a part of or perhaps becomes your conclusion. While there will be applications all through the message, there is one final application of the primary truth which is set forth in your topic. It is not sufficient merely to show what God desires or requires of those who would receive His approval, or even how He makes these things to become operative; but we must show how these things apply to each individual life in a practical outworking in daily experience. People must be made to feel that this particular matter is of supreme importance at the moment, and that God is expecting everyone to act upon it here and now, fully yielding to His claims and expectations in this matter. The *application must be personal,* it must be *practical,* it must be *pertinent.*

I recall hearing, some years ago, a very good sermon on the threefold temptation of Jesus. It was well prepared and ably delivered. The conclusion was excellent, showing that the end never justifies the means. To illustrate, the preacher cited an instance in South America, which was well chosen and very appropriate. Since I happened to be familiar with the conditions existing in that church I could see how well that message fitted the local situation. The preacher had very adroitly brought the truth to bear upon the need and I anticipated his application. He had them "on ice" and there could be no escaping the truth and the necessity of their yielding to it. He had done the job so efficiently that no one could reasonably take offense, no matter how personal the application. My appreciation of his discernment (he had not been there long) and his courage was continually mounting. However, to my surprise and disappointment, he left them stranded in South America. Doubtless the people felt that the principle worked fine in the southern atmosphere and should be adhered to down there, but they were definitely not made to feel that they were flagrantly defying that same principle in their own lives and in their church. They should have been made to feel that the principle demanded immediate conformity on their part, that they could not expect the blessing of God upon their church until they did something about it. He had a conclusion *without* an application, which is a tragedy. "Whatsoever He saith unto you" — conclusion; "do it" — application.

There are many things which need to be simplified and clarified, and this can be done only by use of an illustration. By use of commonplace things spiritual matters difficult to understand will be made understandable and capable of apprehension. Jesus often took the common things of everyday life to illustrate and thus simplify the deep things which so often mystified his listeners: the door, the vine, the branch, the salt, the light, the bread, the water, and many more. Family relationships, agriculture, mechanics, natural science, botany, astronomy, sociology, and various other arts and sciences all contribute splendid illustrative material to give mental pictures of truths that are designed to activate the heart and life. It is well to remember that primarily we are not teaching facts but people. The real test of good preaching is whether or not the people learn anything from the message.

It has already been stated that illustrations should be used sparingly. Present-day preaching is lopsided due to the fact that there is in it such a preponderance of illustrative material. Most modern sermons are from eighty to ninety per cent illustration. Some of them are nothing more than a topic and a collection of illustrations. They do not edify, and have no lasting value.

Expository sermons will require fewer illustrations than others. In some cases you will not use any. That may sound farfetched, but I have seen the most rapt attention at times when there was nothing but pure exposition. It is doubtful if more than twenty-five or thirty per cent of the time should ever be given to illustrations, and usually less than that. Of course that means very thorough preparation and careful description on the part of the preacher.

Above all else there should be the strict avoidance of wearisome details. We have listened to some illustrations that were so long and drawn out that we anticipated both the story and the point before the preacher was half through. *That is boring.* We could not help but feel (whether justly or not) that all this needless detail was just padding to substitute for a lack of real preparation. Condense as much as possible, and hasten on just as quickly as you can to the truth which you are seeking to present. It is true that illustrations are windows which let the light in, but do not make a religious greenhouse out of the pulpit. It then becomes fragile and lacks solidarity. Hothouse plants cannot stand the weather on the outside. Our people need to be "rooted and grounded in love" and in the truth of God, that they shall be "no more children, tossed to and fro, and carried about with every wind of doctrine," and perverted by "the wiles of the devil." They need to "grow up into Him in all things, which is the head, even Christ" (Ephesians 4:14-15). Stories, no matter how fitting or how well told, will never bring that to pass.

Be sure that the stories really illustrate. We have heard most interesting and inspiring incidents related which had no bearing upon the subject matter at all, and did not have any connection with the truth just stated. The preacher had just come across it, or it was fresh in his mind, and he used it. No matter how inspiring or thought-provoking it may be, if the account is irrelevant, it is useless. The same is also true of poetry.

As a rule it is not best to start a message, particularly an exposition, with an illustration, but there are times when this can be done quite effectively. The converse is true concerning the conclusion. One of the very best ways to conclude a message is with a fitting and gripping illustration.

THE PROCLAMATION

There is also the matter of recollection. Sometimes it is difficult to bring to mind the right thing at the right time. Though you have not forgotten it you may not be able to recollect it at the precise moment that it is needed. The use of notes, for this purpose, is something else which needs careful consideration, because it can greatly enhance or detract from the value of the message. There is great need for a proper balance here. We know of a man who can give the entire Scripture passage from memory, and then proceed to deliver a well-planned and powerful message without the sign of a note before him. I wish that it were possible for me to do so, but my mind is not so constructed. We know of another man, one of the nation's most prominent preachers, who takes his sermon almost verbatim into the pulpit with him. However, unless you happened to be sitting in the choir (or were as curious as I am) you would not be likely to know it. His use of notes is so dexterous as to be of no disadvantage to him, nor is it obnoxious to his congregation.

These two men are not representative, they are exceptions. Most men who preach without any notes at all will have a tendency to wander, or to get the cart before the horse. It is difficult for the average man to carry a continuous analytical discourse through a period of thirty minutes or more without notes, unless it happens to be one which he has used often enough to develop thorough familiarity with the message. Likewise, if a man has a manuscript before him he will almost certainly become married to his notes, and lose the attention of his people. There is nothing more provoking than a prolonged pause, while the preacher juts out his chin and gazes through his bifocals, trying to find his place.

There should be at least a skeleton outline, with a few phrases here and there, a pungent statement, an epigram, a quotation, or a note to recall an illustration. The writer has found that one side of half a regular size letterhead is quite sufficient, as a rule. Occasionally there is need for a few extra words on the back. Poems can be on a separate piece of paper, if you do not quote from memory. If you memorize, all you need is the title.

The ideal arrangement is to have a full length manuscript in the file to be consulted beforehand, and a condensed skeleton to take into the pulpit. Even then we should not be bound to those things that we have, brief or otherwise, but leave our minds open for fresh thoughts which will come from God, sometimes on the spur of the moment, and most frequently when we have made thorough and careful preparation.

Much care should be exercised in the use of notes, however brief, so that people will not be conscious of their use. Not that there is any lack of virtue in the use of notes, but an awareness of it is distracting. I was greatly encouraged one time, after having conducted services in a neighboring church for a week. A competent attorney, himself a public speaker and Bible teacher of ability, said, "One thing I appreciated about your preaching was the fact that you do not use any notes." He was amazed when I told him that I had used notes for all but two of the sermons, and said, "Well, I watched carefully, but I could not detect it."

It is not accidental. It is the result of much careful endeavor to develop a technique that will in no way distract or detract from the concentration of the people upon the truth of God which is being presented. In other words we must avoid bringing the workshop into the pulpit.

Finally we might consider the use of the *proposition*. You will wonder why that should be left to the last, because it obviously belongs at the first of this discussion, in the order of things. There is a great deal of difference of opinion on the use of the proposition. Some feel that it is indispensable, that a sermon is crippled without it. Others see no need for it. Not too much has been said on the matter by the specialists. Doubtless many have been using the proposition without particular consideration of it as such, or of its significance. Dr. Whitesell has this to say about it:

> The proposition is the gist of the sermon, the sermon condensed into one sentence, the spinal column running through the message. It is the thing you wish to prove, and becomes the core of the whole message. It is the thing the lawyer states when he begins his plea before a jury; it is the thing the legislator states when he begins to plead for the passage of a favorite measure. It should be stated as an affirmation, or as a question, in one sentence. . . . If a preacher has a good proposition and keeps to it, his message will have unity, progress, clarity, weight, and punch; but if he lacks a proposition, he will flounder and get nowhere. Dr. Charles W. Koller says that the difference between the subject and the proposition is this: "the subject is what you

are going to talk about, the proposition is what you
are going to say about it. The proposition is the sermon in a nutshell."

What the "lead" is to the journalist the proposition is to the preacher. Good journalism calls for a
pithy, catchy, condensed headline, followed by a
concise summary of the whole story, and then the
detailed account. The headline is to create sufficient
curiosity to catch the reader's attention; the lead is to
develop enough interest in the story to make the
reader want to know all of the facts in the case.

So it is with the proposition. It whets the appetite
of the hearers, so that they will want to follow on to
discover how these things can be deduced, how they
can be substantiated, and what is the significance of
the ultimate conclusion. The proposition will usually
come immediately after the topic, but it may follow
the introduction, depending upon the content or
length of the introduction. In one sense it should be
incorporated in the introduction.

It may seem that there is a host of constituent
elements in a sermon; but most preachers have these
various parts to their sermons, whether or not they
have given it special consideration, or diagnosed and
pigeonholed each part. There must be a blending of
these elements into a smoothly flowing stream of
spiritual truth that will charm the audience into
humble and sincere obedience to the divine purpose.

We usually wish to include a Scripture reading in
the opening exercises of the service. If the passage

under consideration is relatively short, as in the case of Zacchaeus, one should read the entire account. If the passage contains more than ten or twelve verses, it may be best to select a pertinent paragraph within the passage, which would be of reasonable length, than to read the entire passage. Sometimes it is best to reduce it to three or four verses. If there is a section to which you intend to give major emphasis, read that. It will have a tendency to cause the listeners to start thinking along that line before you actually launch into your sermon. The selected reading does not have to be taken from the first part of the chapter or passage, it may be in the middle or at the conclusion. This in itself may provoke some curiosity and forethought.

CHAPTER 6

THE OUTGROWTH OF EXPOSITION

THE PRACTICAL CLINIC

CLOSED CIRCUIT TELEVISION is being used extensively in many educational institutions in this day of electronic contrivances. Suppose we set up a hidden camera in the expositor's study, so that we can monitor his procedures without causing him any distraction, as he begins to prepare his messages for next Sunday. This is Tuesday morning. By remote control we may be able to discover some helpful hints which could enable us to get off to a good start in the realm of expository preaching.

This particular expositor endeavors to avoid sermon preparation on Mondays; he stays out of his study, and away from his books as much as possible, trying to find some diversion which will relieve and renew his mental capacities. This is Tuesday morning, and he plans to stay with it for three or four hours each morning through Saturday. He finds himself in agreement with Dr. Gerald Kennedy, who said, "A steady habit of at least four hours a day of study is the only foundation upon which you can build an adequate preparation of sermons."

This expositor is engaged in a series of sermons on the Gospel of Luke. Last Sunday he preached on "The Significance of the Sabbath" (Luke 6:1-5). Next Sunday he will confine himself to Luke 6:6-11. He takes a sheet of notepaper and starts out in this manner:

Verse 6. "Entered . . . snyagogue" — He set a good example concerning devotion to the appointed place of worship. "Taught" — people need to be instructed in the ways of righteousness. Worship involves learning as well as inspiration. "There was a man" — he was in the right place, at the right time, to receive the help that he needed. Attending church does not save, but may result in conversion. "Right hand was withered" — his best hand was crippled, he could not help himself, nobody else could relieve the situation for him. The One who could provide the remedy was there. He is always present when a soul wants to do business with God.

Verse 7. "Watched Him" — critically. They were there to find fault, to condemn Him if He dared to help this man. "Heal on the sabbath" — the day, and their religious code and traditions, were more important than worship or the blessing of others. They did not *want* to be enlightened, they only sought grounds for "an accusation." Those who should have been supporting Him, and cooperating with Him, were out to destroy Him. They were spiritually crippled, and just as needy in spirit as the physically handicapped man.

Verse 8. "He knew their thoughts" — going

beyond ESP. God only can peer into the human soul. This would have convinced them if their minds had been open to truth. "Rise up, and stand forth"—He deliberately created the issue—He challenged them. He did not compromise or take a more amiable course of procedure, to avoid a crisis, or protect Himself. Not the easy way. "He arose and stood forth"—astounded probably, frightened, fearful, wondering, but he acted upon the instruction. Not reasoning, questioning, doubting, no logic applied—he just took Jesus at His word, and acted. That is faith. If he had debated he might have missed the greatest experience of his life. He simply obeyed.

Verse 9. His critics knew what to expect, they knew He would extend mercy. They were aware of His character, but ignored His person. "I will ask you one thing"—not just defiance, they must know *why* He will perform the miracle. They must see that He alone can provide the spiritual healing which they need so much. "Is it lawful . . . to do good . . . to save life?"—what better use of the sabbath than to deliver a handicapped man? (Check Matthew 12:9-12—critics were inconsistent, placing more value on a sheep than a man—good illustration). Failure to do *good* is a sin. They do not *want* to see, therefore *cannot* be helped. (Mark 3:4—"they held their peace.") To reply would expose their infidelity, hypocrisy, and treachery.

Verse 10. "Looking . . . upon them all"—not at the cripple, but at the critics. Challenging with His eyes, daring them to question the correctness of what He is about to do. (Check Mark 3:5.) Let them show evidence why this man should *not* be restored. Petty criticism is inconsistent and groundless. "Stretch forth thy hand"—a direct command. "And he did so" — he did what he could *not* do. No hesitation, no question, no complaint, no expression of weakness or inadequacy. No logical reasoning or psychological thinking. He just did it. His response brought about the miracle. "Restored whole as the other" — an instantaneous and total restoration, not a gradual process. Jesus does a complete job when He is obeyed. Not just temporary alleviation or improvement.

Verse 11. "Filled with madness" — it should have been gladness. A miracle, a restoration, a man delivered, a life changed, rejoicing, a home blessed — none of this means a thing to biased critics. "Communed . . . what they might do to Jesus" (Matthew 12:14). He interfered with their concepts, codes, traditions, and programs, so He must go, be liquidated. (Spirit of communism.) Should have fallen on their knees in repentance, seeking forgiveness and pledging allegiance to their Messiah. They plot to destroy Him. They never ceased until they nailed Him to the cross. Does He get in your way?

The expositor has pretty well exhausted his own thinking on this passage, for the time being, so now he turns to other translations and word studies. These will be identified as follows: *Amp* — the Amplified Bible. *Berk* — the Berkeley Version. *LB* — the Living Bible. *Rieu* — C. H. Rieu. *NEB* — the New English Bible. *Gspd* — Goodspeed. *Wuest* — Kenneth Wuest's word studies (Mark). *Vin* — Vincent's word studies. *Vine* — Vine's Greek Dictionary. *Strong* — Exhaustive Concordance. *Wms* — Williams New Testament.

Luke 6, verse 7. "In order that they might get [some ground for] an accusation against Him" (Amp). "Eager to find some charge" (LB). "So they might trump up some charge against Him" (Berk). "They kept on watching Him, bent on finding our Lord at fault with reference to the sabbath." "They were watching Him carefully and closely, as one who dogs another's steps" (Wuest). "Wycliffe translates 'They espieden Him' that is, they played the spy. Accuse means to accuse formally and before a tribunal, to bring a charge publicly" (Wuest — Mark). "Whether He is actually healing" (Vin).

Verse 8. "Aware all along of their thought" (Amp). "How well He knew their thoughts" (LB). "Come and stand here where everyone can see" (LB). "So he got up, and stood there" (Wms).

Verse 9. "I put the question to you" (NEB). "Are we permitted on the sabbath to choose between doing good and doing evil?" (Rieu) "To do good (so that someone derives advantage from it) or to do evil? To save a life (and make a soul safe) or to destroy it?" (Amp)
"Therein essentially lay the difference between Him and the Pharisees, in whose theory and practice, religious duty and benevolence, the divine and the human, were divorced." "To omit to do good in your power is evil; not to save life when you can, is to destroy it" (Wuest — Mark 3:4). "They held their peace — they kept on being quiet." "Theirs was a painful and embarrassing silence" (Wuest).

Verse 10. "He looked around at them one by one" (LB). (Personal soul-searching.) "Fully restored" (Amp). "Completely normal" (LB). "Restored" — "of restoration to a former condition of health"

(Vine). "To reconstitute (in health, home, or organization)" (Strong).

Verse 11. "They were filled with lack of understanding and senseless rage, and discussed (consulted) with one another" (Amp). "Wild with rage, and began to plot His murder" (LB). "Beside themselves with anger" (NEB). "Perfectly furious" (Gspd). (Check Greek further on this.) "Senseless rage, as distinguished from intelligent indignation" (Vine). (Check Matthew 12:14.)

When the expositor came to the phrase, "Stretch forth thy hand," an idea for a topic popped into his mind. So many in these days are seeking something for nothing, so a topic like "The Handout" should attract attention. The withered hand is the central focus of the whole passage anyway. He then began to work on the main divisions of the outline. How did the handout come about? What took place? What followed? So the outline began to take shape.

Topic—"The Handout."
1. The *occasion* for it (verses 6-7). Cripple in the synagogue needing help. Hypocrites in the synagogue, purposing to hurt.

2. The *operation* of it (verses 8-9). Deity can plumb the depths of the soul and challenge the conscience. Issue created, inner protests silenced. Stage is set.

3. The *outcome* of it (verses 10-11). The look of authority. The command. The response—immediate. The resentment and rejection—also immediate.

Having the topic and the main divisions of his outline defined, the expositor now turns to his commentaries and volumes of sermons for further research. As he pursues this part of his preparation he finds that he has already reached many of the conclusions stated by the different authors, and this is encouraging. Here and there he catches a new gleam of light, or some spiritual gem, which he had not unearthed for himself. Some helpful parallels are set forth, and some practical applications are suggested. A pertinent piece of poetry is fitting, so he decides to incorporate that in the sermon.

Although the reading of so many pages has resulted in a great deal of repetition, and much material seems to be obvious (or even superficial), the constant coverage of the passage has indelibly stamped the truths contained therein on his mind, until he has a graphic picture of the scene before his mind's eye continually. Before the week is over he is *actually living with it*. Some of the research has been rather tedious and sometimes wearisome, but it has activated his mind — pro and con — until he has pretty well mastered the passage. Now he can hardly wait until Sunday to go into the pulpit and share these blessed truths with his congregation.

Having completed his research, the expositor now goes back to the completion of his outline. It will be noticed that he condensed his findings into terse, brief, pithy statements, which will be sufficient to recall to his mind the truths which he will endeavor to impart to his people. Some of the things which he has discovered for his own enlightenment and edification will not be preached at this time. Some things which unraveled slowly will be summarized briefly, others will be enlarged upon and emphasized. The following is the outline, and notes which the expositor will take into the pulpit on Sunday.

THE HANDOUT — Luke 6:6-11

1. THE OCCASION FOR IT

The Disability Evidenced — verse 6.

Jesus was there, a consistent example. "Taught" — instruction essential. The cripple was there. We must see that they get to Jesus. "*Right* hand" — man's best still no good. Jesus alone can solve our problems.

The Disloyalty Encountered — verse 7.

The critics were there. "Watched Him" — to find fault, to destroy. Not seeking enlightenment, just grounds for accusation, condemnation. They should have been cooperating and supporting Him. Willingly, and spiritually crippled. "None so blind as he who *will not* see." Better be a cripple than a critic.

2. THE OPERATION OF IT

The Insight Revealed — verse 8.

"Knew their thoughts" — Deity can perceive inward duplicity, read the conscience. Honesty would have convinced them of His deity. "Rise up, and stand forth" — the issue is created — hypocrisy is challenged. He will not protect Himself at the expense of the cripple. One cripple more important than a host of critics, or even His own life.

The Intention Resented—verse 9.

A fair question. Only God answers questions before they are asked. This would have convinced them if they were sincere. *Matthew 12:9-12.* Inconsistent in unbelief, a sheep more important than a man. They do not *want* to see, so they *cannot* be helped. *Mark 3:4*—"they held their peace." A reply would expose their unreasonable infidelity and treachery.

3. THE OUTCOME OF IT

The Command Presented—verse 10.

"He looked around at them one by one" (LB). Personal—soul-searching. Looking at the critics, not the cripple. Withering, challenging, daring, defying them to question His authority to act on behalf of the cripple. Petty criticism is always groundless. "Stretch forth thy hand"—a positive and direct command. "And he did so"—no question, no argument, no excuse, no explanation desired. He just obeyed—he did it—*now.* Did what he could not do, at His command. No reasoning, no doubting. He simply did *what he was told to do,* doubtless to his own amazement. His response projected the miracle. "Restored"—instantaneously, totally—"as the other"—permanently. Picture of conversion, not just improvement, or alleviation, but regeneration.

The Commotion Provoked—verse 11.

Jesus constantly created commotions. "Filled with madness"—"senseless rage"—"perfectly furious"—"insane fury." Not even intelligent. Should have been rejoicing immensely. The cripple is ignored. Total selfishness. Dogmas and traditions come first. Jesus must be removed.

Is He in your way?—Matthew 12:14—"held a council against Him, how they might destroy Him." They never ceased until He was nailed to the cross. That cripple cost Him his life. Has your testimony cost you anything?

Final application. "And he did so." Are you going to do so? Whatever it is He is demanding of you, you had better do it now. Closing illustration.

The message is not profound, it involves no real problems of exegesis. The outline is simplicity itself, but will enable the expositor to move along smoothly and coherently. A few brief remarks about the other sabbath (verses 1-5) would be appropriate as an introduction. The restoration can apply to the conversion experience, or it can apply to Christians who have "dried up on the stalk," so to speak.

The final application might also be made from verse 11, showing the deadly evil of unbelief. Rejection on the part of unbelievers, or disobedience on the part of Christians. Either is despicable. Either "madness" or "gladness." Or the final application could be made from verse 8. Christians need to stand up and be counted. Sinners need to take their stand for Jesus.

There are other topics suggested by the account. "A cripple or a critic?" "Where do you stand?" or "No middle ground." It will be noted that the outline is alliterative. This is not essential but it can be beneficial. Alliteration comes easy to this author. If that is not true of the reader it might be well to leave it alone. As long as the wording of the heading summarizes the content of that portion of Scripture, and enables you to move effectively from one point to the next one, that is what counts. Each heading should lead to a further unfolding of the truth incorporated in the topic.

There is this to be said in favor of alliteration. It does serve to enlarge and enhance your vocabulary. In order to find the right word, to match the others, you must necessarily know exactly what you are seeking to describe, thus insuring the accuracy of your preaching. I would suggest that you use alliteration if it helps you, ignore it if it hinders you.

It is now Saturday morning, and the expositor has just typed up his notes for pulpit use, on a half page of regular letterhead. His notes are sufficient to recall what he intends to say, but not so cumbersome as to get bogged down. He will be able to speak extemporaneously and maintain the attention and interest of his people, without having to read from a manuscript, and without the danger of becoming confused. He will neither wander nor wane.

He needs a good heart-touching illustration to conclude his message — a real clincher — so he goes to his file and finds a clipping which he had set aside for this purpose. It went like this:

Dr. Howerton told of an old slave in North Carolina, who could not read. He sent for Dr. Howerton, and asked him to read John 3:16 for him. Then he said: "Marse Jim, sign my name to that verse, and let me tech de pen." "Uncle Charlie" had a little lot and cabin deeded to him, and he understood the legalities of making a contract when one could not read or write. When he was dying Charlie was wont to say, "I ain't got nothing to do to be saved but to believe on Jesus, and I done signed the Bible to show dat I do." Have you reached out with the hand of faith and "teched the pen"?

Tomorrow morning the expositor will come into his study and go over his notes, formulating in his mind the things that he plans to say when he goes into the pulpit. Some of those things may not be said, and some things may come to his mind, on the spur of the moment, which he had not planned to say. Of course that would not be so, had he not done diligent preparation during the week. God will never bless presumption.

Now the expositor drops to his knees to commit the whole matter to Him who wrote the Book, the One who had called him to preach His Word, "putting (him) into the ministry."

It is time to disconnect the camera, and hasten to our own study. Hungry hearts are waiting, we must not — we dare not — disappoint them.

Variety is desirable in expository preaching. Luke 15 lends itself very well, to illustrate this feature. There are several ways in which this chapter may be treated. One might take the four facets of this parable, and treat each one separately, over an extended period of time, without any reference to the remainder of the chapter. It would not even be necessary to take them in order. Each message would be complete in itself, and would serve to meet the need of the hour at that time. Since there would be no theme, the topics might run as follows: 1. "Find That Sheep" or "Hang In There." 2. "Keep That Lamp Lit" or "Home Economics." 3. "Come On Home" or "His Father Ran." 4. "The Prodigal Who Stayed Home" or "Stop Whining."

At a later date, even in the same pastorate, a series of messages could be developed. The general theme could be "Heavenly Outreach." Under the theme the messages might take this order: verses 1-7 — "Divine Pursuit"; verses 8-10 — "Determined Persistence"; verses 11-24 — "Delightful Possession"; verses 25-32 — "Degenerate Pouting."

Again, the entire chapter may be covered in one message, under the topic "God Seeks Man" or "Seeking the Lost." Verses 1-7 — "God in Christ *redeeming* the sinner." The sheep depicts a *bewildered* sinner. Verses 8-10 — "God in the Holy Spirit *retrieving* the sinner." The coin depicts an *unconscious* sinner. Verses 11-32 — "God the Father *reclaiming* the sinner." The lost son depicts a *willful* sinner. Whether or not the parable is intended to convey the fact that all three persons of the Godhead are active in the redemption of lost men, the parable lends itself justifiably to such an adaption.

The last division could have a dual thrust, using both sons, or the message could conclude with the wayward son. One penitent son, and one impenitent son. Both belong to the Father by generation, but only one by regeneration. Up-and-outs are very often more difficult to reach than the down-and-outs. Since there is such an abundance of material it might be better to eliminate the pharasaical son. In either case it will be necessary to move rapidly from one picture to another, to avoid becoming tedious and wearisome.

This just serves to point up the way that many passages of Scripture may be treated, at various times, to obtain variety in expository preaching. It is not necessary to revert to topical or textual preaching in order to secure variety in preaching. Nevertheless, it would not be wise to tackle that whole chapter until there are several years of experience to back it up.

Very often the same passage can be treated at a much later date, with an entirely different thrust. The author preached on a passage early in his ministry, and then discovered several years later, that he had developed a second sermon (with a new topic, and a new outline), without being aware of having preached on that passage previously. That was before he developed a system of filing his sermon notes. In fact it was in the process of developing the system that he discovered this.

THE ANALYTICAL EXHIBIT

Perhaps the best way to portray, in a practical and understandable manner, the principles previously set forth is to offer some specimens of skeleton outlines and expository analysis. These are not chosen because of their literary excellence, or because they are superior in this category, but rather because of their simplicity and objectivity. They are representative and exemplary, according to their adaptability. They are practical in that they have been tried and tested, and have been used with satisfactory results. Where not otherwise credited they are the product of the author, devised, and possibly revised, over a long period of years. First of all we shall consider expositions of single passages of Scripture, without any connection to other passages.

To begin with, we shall take a passage with only two main divisions. The passage is Genesis 35:1-15. The sermon topic is UNDER THE OAK.

1. *The Oak of Compromise* (verse 4).
2. *The Oak of Consecration* (verse 8).

The two trees seem to figure prominently in this passage, thus the passage may be developed around these two verses. One might use some subheadings, but in this case we shall not do that.

The Oak of Compromise. The first seven verses set forth a picture of compromise. The preceding chapter shows the disastrous results of this compromise, with all its vileness. Then comes the call back to Bethel, and the wise decision to go. Bethel was where Jacob had left God. God never leaves us, He simply declines to be a part of our compromise, so we must get back to the point where we left Him in our experience. Then the symbols of carnality and backsliding were buried in a conspicuous place, where they could be easily recovered, in case they did not go through with their determination to return to God. "Make not provision for the flesh" (Romans 13:14).

The Oak of Consecration. The last eight verses in the passage speak of consecration. They did return to Bethel. It is well to commemorate and mark clearly the resting place of a godly and devout person such as Deborah. This is the sort of thing that we need to recall over and over again, for our inspiration and encouragement.

If subheadings seem to be desirable, from one to three under each main heading would be appropriate.

Now let us consider a passage with three main divisions. The passage is John 21:1-25. The topic is LEADERSHIP.

1. HUMAN LEADERSHIP — verses 1-5
   The Frailty of It
   Peter was just the spokesman for the group. All they needed was someone to suggest that they return to the boats.
   The Fruitlessness of It
   They caught "nothing" and were required to acknowledge their failure.

2. DIVINE LEADERSHIP — verses 6-11
   Demands Obedience
   "The right side of the ship" is the side of His choosing. That is the "side" that always brings blessing and success.
   Delivers Abundance
   "The multitude of fishes" — "dragging the net with fishes" — "Bring of the fish which ye have now caught." Superabundance follows the night of failure, and they are to partake of the provision first of all.

3. SPIRIT-FILLED LEADERSHIP—verses 12-25
The Fresh Commission
There was a humbling experience, but it was done so graciously. There was no rejection, but a new commission. Not repudiation but renewal. Through Peter, the spokesman, to all the others.

The Final Consecration
Peter is notified of the suffering which is ahead, and the termination of his life. He is not to be governed by what happens to others, or what they may do. Just live and die for Jesus. "Follow Me" is the mandate for all, and for all time.

Dr. Griffith Thomas was an analytical expert, and this skeleton outline from his pen is lucid. The Scripture is Psalm 16:1-11.

THE LIFE OF THE BELIEVER

1. Its Commencement (verses 1-4)
2. Its Course (verses 5-8)
3. Its Culmination (verses 9-11)

Some passages seem to lend themselves to a fourfold division of the material. The experience in the life of David recorded in 1 Chronicles 21:1-30 could be treated in this way. (Note 2 Samuel 24.)

THE PRIDE OF LIFE

1. THE TRANSGRESSION OF PRIDE—verses 1-7

David Was Inflated by Success
Satan provoked him to take a census of Israel "that I may know" what a great people this is. It is sufficient for God to know that.

David Was Impervious to Suggestion

Though Joab was not outstanding for his spirituality he gave David some very practical advice on this occasion, but David was determined to have his own way "and God was displeased with this."

2. THE CONFESSION OF PRIDE—verses 8-13

The Sincerity of His Confession

It has been said that the three hardest words in human speech are "I was wrong." David was not too proud to make such an acknowledgment when God disciplined the people. "I have sinned greatly"—"do away the iniquity of Thy servant"—"I have done very foolishly." He seeks immediate correction of the situation.

The Sensitivity of His Confession

Two of the suggested disciplines would be unlikely to touch the king to any appreciable degree, so he chose the one most likely to include himself. Also it would be of comparatively short duration, and would put them all in the hands of their merciful God. He would not choose that which would be to his own advantage.

3. THE RETRIBUTION OF PRIDE—verses 14-17

This Is Inevitable

The law of moral retribution demands that we shall reap what we sow. There was no escaping the pestilence, but it could be alleviated. Retribution may be tempered with mercy if there is a genuine penitence.

This Is Indispensable

Retribution will bring people to their senses and to their knees. To escape punitive action would not be a deterrent for the future. God is concerned about our entire life. When David made it clear that he was ready to take upon himself the rest of the chastening, God relaxed the severity of it.

4. THE ABOLITION OF PRIDE — verses 18-27
There Was Obedient Devotion

David was quick to follow instruction, both as to the place and the exercise. He is ready to secure it "for the full price" for this important expression of devotion to God.

There Was Overwhelming Dedication

"I will not take that which is thine for the LORD, nor offer burnt offerings without cost." That which costs nothing is worth nothing. We have not worshiped, nor have we proved our devotion to God, until it has cost us something. That spirit will abolish all pride. In the light of such devotion and dedication "The LORD commanded the angel; and he put up his sword."

Dr. J. O. Williams was another excellent analyst, and he suggested this four-point outline on Psalm 111:1-10:

PRAISE FOR THE WORKS OF GOD

1. God's Works Are Great (verse 2)
2. God's Works Are Glorious (verse 3)
3. God's Works Are Genuine (verse 7)
4. God's Works Are Gracious (verse 9)

There are times when a passage of Scripture seems to rotate around one verse or statement in the passage. An example of this would be found in

Psalm 51. The pivot verse is verse 10; "Create in me a clean heart, O God; and renew a right spirit within me." The rest of the psalm may be developed around that statement.

THE REVIVAL PRAYER

1. The Repentance Expressed (verses 1-9)
2. The Rededication Experienced (verses 11-12)
3. The Renewal Expected (verses 13-19)

Another passage which could be treated in like manner, with a four-point outline, is Numbers 31:1-32. Verse 6 is the pivot verse, and the entire passage would be developed around the question, "Shall your brethren go to war, and shall ye sit here?"

THE BURNING QUESTION

1. THE OCCASION FOR IT (verses 1-6)
   Sluggishness
   Selfishness

2. THE REASON FOR IT (verses 7-15)
   Discouragement
   Detriment

3. THE SACRIFICE INVOLVED IN IT   (verses 16-22)
   No Reluctance
   No Reservation

4. THE CHALLENGE CONTAINED IN IT
(verses 23-32)
It Is Inescapable
It Is Irresistible

It is possible to cover an entire book of the Bible in one expository sermon, in a comprehensive manner. Obviously, the longer the book the more difficult it is to do. To be proficient it would be better to stay with the shorter books.

The writer does not know where this originated, but many years ago someone came up with an outline for the book of Jonah:

A MAN ON THE RUN

1. Running Away from God (chapter 1)
2. Running to God (chapter 2)
3. Running with God (chapter 3)
4. Running Ahead of God (chapter 4)

I have used this message as stated, and have also presented a series of four messages, under the general theme, *A Man on the Run*.

The book of Philippians lends itself quite readily to a similar treatment. Again, this can be treated in a series of four messages, under the same general heading.

THE BELIEVER'S JOY

1. Joy in Captivity (chapter 1)
2. Joy in Humility (chapter 2)

3. Joy in Adversity (chapter 3)
4. Joy in Anxiety (chapter 4)

It is more difficult to prepare the message on Philippians than on Jonah, because there is so much doctrine in the former, while the book of Jonah is purely narrative. The book of Ruth would be easier to handle, for the same reason.

In conclusion we shall consider the matter of *consecutive exposition*. This we believe to be the crown jewel of expositional excellence. *This is the cream of all preaching*. The expositor will not start out his ministry with a consecutive series, if he is wise. When he does decide to present a series covering an entire book of the Bible, it had better not be Romans or Revelation. The Gospel according to Mark would be a good place to start. It is shorter than the other Gospels, is systematically set forth (which is not true of Luke), and is written from the standpoint of service; therefore it seems to pose less theological difficulties.

If this treatment is a new experience for the expositor he may prefer to present a miscellaneous series of messages, without a general theme. If he does wish to pursue a specific theme it will be necessary to do quite a bit of preparatory work before launching into the series. The following thematic series was found to be quite satisfactory. The recognized key verse to the Gospel of Mark is: "For even the Son of man came not to be ministered unto, but to minister, and to give His life a ransom for many" (Mark 10:45). This statement provides the source of the theme.

THE SERVANT OF ALL

1. The Servant Appears (1:1-20)
2. The Servant at Work (1:21-45)
3. The Servant in Conflict (2)
4. The Servant and Opposition (3)
5. The Servant Instructs (4:1-34)
6. The Servant Is Master (4:35 — 5:43)
7. The Servant Meets Unbelief (6)
8. The Servant Extends Mercy (7)
9. The Servant Treats Blindness (8:1-26)
10. The Servant Seeks Confession (8:27 — 9:13)
11. The Servant Tests Character (9:14-50)
12. The Servant Answers Questions (10)
13. The Servant Asserts Authority (11)
14. The Servant Exposes Hypocrisy (12)
15. The Servant Predicts the Future (13)
16. The Servant in the Shadows (14:1-26)
17. The Servant Is Tried (14:27 — 15:15)
18. The Servant Is Dead (15:16-41)
19. The Servant Is Alive (15:42 — 16:20)

The topic of sermon number six should create interest and speculation, since it is in the form of a paradox. Of course only one Servant can be master, and He is master in every situation. He is master in three realms, all of which are beyond our control; we cannot cope with them. Therefore He is master of every situation in which we may find ourselves. The message was outlined as follows:

THE SERVANT IS MASTER

1. HE IS MASTER IN THE NATURAL REALM
   The Tempest (verses 35-37)
   The Terror (verses 38-41)

2. HE IS MASTER IN THE SPIRITUAL REALM
   The Dominance (5:1-5)
   The Deliverance (verses 6-20)

3. HE IS MASTER IN THE PHYSICAL REALM
   The Disease (verses 25-34)
   The Decease (verses 21-24 — [interlude] — 35-43)

Dr. Russell Bradley Jones developed a series covering the First Epistle to the Corinthians, following a specific theme:

A PURIFIED CHURCH

1. The Possession of the Church: the Power of God (1:1-9)
2. The Peril of the Church: a Divided Christ (1:10-16)
3. The Proclamation of the Church: Christ, the Power and Wisdom of God (1:17 — 2:16)
4. The Purpose of the Church: Building for Fire (3:1-23)
5. The Pleasure of the Church: Fools for Christ's Sake (4:1-21)
6. The Pollution of the Church: Sores in the Christian Body (5:1 — 6:20)
7. The Peculiarity of the Church: Separation unto Christ (7:1 — 8:13)

8. The Problems of the Church: the World, the Flesh, and the Devil (9:1 — 12:31)
9. The Prerequisite of the Church: Unfailing Love (13:1-13)
10. The Privilege of the Church: Identification with Christ (14:1 — 16:24)

This series was developed in the days when we used to have revival campaigns which lasted for two weeks, with services each weekday morning, Monday through Friday. This series would be used at the morning hour. Some of the messages cover a great deal of material, and would be difficult to present at a regular morning service on Sunday morning. This is particularly true of sermons eight and ten. It might be better to develop a series of twelve or more sermons, following the same general theme and procedure.

Another series on First Corinthians was developed by Dr. K. Owen White. He did not follow a theme, but gave a miscellaneous series, Sunday by Sunday. This would be the same as a number of separate expositions, only it did cover a whole book, and they were delivered consecutively. He has some very interesting topics (particularly ten and fifteen) though they are unrelated.

1. Christ — the Power and Wisdom of God
2. The Only Message
3. The Church's One Foundation
4. Humiliation That Leads to Glory
5. The Leaven of Immorality
6. Dishonoring God in Your Body

7. The Glory of a Christian Home
8. My Personal Responsibility
9. That I Might by All Means Save Some
10. When Temptation Takes You
11. Understanding and Appreciating the Lord's Supper
12. What Is Your Spiritual Gift?
13. The More Excellent Way
14. An Uncertain Sound
15. Death Defied and Defeated
16. The Great Door and the Many Adversaries

It will be noticed that he followed the chapter divisions all the way through, since he was not confined to a specific number of sermons.

Another series, with a specific theme, covers the First Epistle of Peter:

THE SUFFERINGS OF THE SAINTS

1. Rejoicing — the Antidote to Suffering (1:1-9)
2. Holiness — the Product of Suffering (1:10-25)
3. Growth — the Outcome of Suffering (2:1-10)
4. Submission — the Strength of Suffering (2:11-25)
5. Subjection — the Beauty of Suffering (3:1-22)
6. Victory — the Value of Suffering (4:1-11)
7. Participation — the Satisfaction of Suffering (4:12-19)
8. Perfection — the End of Suffering (5:1-11)

Each message is complete in itself, but is definitely and closely linked to the theme, as well as coinciding with the other messages.

A longer series, covering a much larger book of the Bible, can also be developed under a given theme. In this series on the book of Acts each message is tied in with the theme, though there is no particular continuity of thought in the messages themselves, other than the fact that the material has to do with the formulation and continuance of the local church.

THE NEW TESTAMENT CHURCH IN ACTION

1. The Mobilization of the Church (1:1-26)
2. The Regimentation of the Church (2:1-47)
3. The Aggression of the Church (3:1 — 4:4)
4. The Crises of the Church (4:5-31)
5. The Power of the Church (4:32 — 5:42)
6. The Fellowship of the Church (6:1-15)
7. The Pedigree of the Church (7:1-60)
8. The Expansion of the Church (8:1-40)
9. The Triumphs of the Church (9:1-43)
10. The Universality of the Church (10:1-48)
11. The Development of the Church (11:1-30)
12. The Strength of the Church (12:1-25)
13. The Extension of the Church (13:1-52)
14. The Perseverance of the Church (14:1-28)
15. The Indoctrination of the Church (15:1-41)
16. The Outreach of the Church (16:1-40)
17. The Persistence of the Church (17:1-34)
18. The Progression of the Church (18:1-28)
19. The Prevalence of the Church (19:1-41)
20. The Edification of the Church (20:1-38)
21. The Dynamic of the Church (21:1-40)
22. The Declaration of the Church (22:1-30)

23. The Consolation of the Church (23:1-35)
24. The Examination of the Church (24:1-27)
25. The Defense of the Church (25:1-27)
26. The Witness of the Church (26:1-32)
27. The Endurance of the Church (27:1-44)
28. The Steadfastness of the Church (28:1-31)

Dr. J. C. Macauley is a master of analysis, and holds almost exclusively to the threefold division. The following samples are superb:

Scripture: Acts 5:1-21

THE GHOST OF ACHAN

1. The Sin That Threatened the Church
2. The Severity That Saved the Church
3. The Sanctity That Glorified the Church

Scripture: Acts 11:19-30; 12:25

AS FAR AS ANTIOCH

1. The Origin of a Gentile Church
2. The Ordering of a Gentile Church
3. The Offering of a Gentile Church

Scripture: Acts 16:11-34

THE ASSAULT ON EUROPE

1. A Beachhead Secured
2. A Counterattack Instigated
3. An Offensive Launched

Scripture: Acts 22:17-22

PAUL RECALLS AN ARGUMENT

1. How Paul Perceived the Will of God
2. How Paul Protested the Will of God
3. How Paul Pursued the Will of God

THE FINISHED PRODUCT

The following sermon is submitted merely as an example. There is nothing of great significance about it. It is complete in itself, but could easily be included in a series of historical expositions on the second book of Kings. The message deals with the matter of revival, and is directed toward the Christian community. Other topics could be used, and possibly with more significance. However, the author felt that the whole point of the message is the fact that, with all of the preparatory work that was done, which is designed to create an atmosphere for revival, they really *did not* have the sort of revival which might have been expected — hence the topic.

This message has been delivered more than once, and the outline has been revised a little each time. The content is basically the same. We hope that it will exemplify, to some extent at least, the matter which this book endeavors to encompass.

NOTWITHSTANDING
2 Kings 22 — 23

These chapters provide us with an account of the

revival under Josiah, king of Judah. Despite the fact that both his father and grandfather were vile and wicked men, who "did that which was evil in the sight of the LORD" — "served the idols . . . worshipped them" and "walked not in the way of the LORD" (2 Kings 21:20-22), Josiah was a godly man, who "did that which was right in the sight of the LORD, and walked in all the way of David his father [ancestor], and turned not aside to the right hand or to the left" (2 Kings 22:2). This indicates that a man can overcome his heritage and environment, if he so desires, and will permit God to direct his life.

1. THE RENOVATION FOR REVIVAL

Restoration—of the Word of God

At the early age of twenty-six Josiah began the huge task of repairing the Temple of God. For about two hundred and fifty years the sanctuary had been in a state of negligence and disrepair. If things deteriorated as fast then as they do now, the condition of God's house must have been pitiful. Spiritually speaking I doubt if it was in much worse condition than some of our religious mausoleums are now. Launching a movement for spiritual renewal in most of our modern churches today would not get the response which Josiah did.

However the procedure seems not to be too different then than now, when it comes to a building program. I doubt if they had as many committees, or took as long to get started, but they made it clear that the work was to be financed by "the silver which is brought into the house of the LORD, which the keepers of the door [ushers?] have gathered of the people" (verse 4). The cash was to be delivered to those who had been employed to do the work, and there was no bookkeeping, no performance bond, and no contract to sign, with no deed of trust at the bank. One thing can definitely be said in favor of the workmen back then, "they dealt faithfully." I wish that were true of all church members today, to say nothing of the ungodly.

When they started the work of repair on the house of God they discovered the Bible. It was only the first five books of the Old Testament, at the most, and they did not know what it was, but they knew it must have some significance. [Despite the fact that today every dime store in the country has a stack of Bibles for sale, at a price that anyone can afford, a great multitude of people, including church members, do not know what it is all about. They may have it on the shelf at home, or even on the coffee table (if they think the pastor might call), but the content might just as well be in the original tongues, so far as their knowledge and understanding of it is concerned.] When they went to *work* in the house of God they found the *Word* of God. The vast majority of professing Christians need to get back into fellowship with God in living experience. The Bible is a misplaced book in the personal life, the domestic life, and even the church life, of the majority of our Chrisitian families today.

Realization—of the Truth of God

The high priest apparently could not read (reading was a rare privilege in those days) so he delivered the book to Shaphan the scribe, who read it and then delivered it to the king, after giving him a report on the book. The king requested him to read the book to him. The king not only recognized the divine origin of the book, but was ready to accept it at face value, and gave outward evidence of his acceptance of the truth by rending his clothes. This was the manner by which humility and penitence was manifested. In these days it is well nigh impossible to get a church member to *admit* there is anything wrong, much less acknowledge it.

Josiah did not pass it on to someone else, but took the matter to heart, applying the truth to his own life, and to that of his people. There was no argument, no hesitation, no minimizing, no "it could be worse" attitude. There was just a definite realization of guilt and unworthiness. How refreshing it would be to see such open sincerity today, without probing, stabbing, and constant berating.

"Go ye, inquire of the LORD for me, and for the people" was the command. "For great is the *wrath* of the LORD that is kindled against us, because our fathers have not hearkened unto the words of this book" (verse 13). It would have been so easy to blame his ancestors, and settle down with the status quo. So many would simply say, "This is not relevant to our day," and forget about it. It was not so with Josiah. He was frightened at what he found in the book, and he wanted to find out what could be done to avert the promised disaster. When we see, plainly stated, God's hatred of sin and disobedience, it *should* strike terror to our hearts.

2. THE REGULATION FOR REVIVAL

Revelation

It appears that Jeremiah was not in close proximity, and there being no other man on the scene who was in close enough touch with God to give the needed interpretation, the Lord used a godly woman to do it. When He cannot proceed through the regular channels, God will find another way to get His truth to those who want to know it. When we sincerely show a desire to have His truth, it will be made available to us. The trouble today is that too many people seem to be doing their best to avoid it, and show resentment or cold indifference when it is presented to them.

The interpretation is easily understood, but is not very comforting. "Thus saith the LORD, Behold, I will bring evil upon this place" because of their shameful idolatry and "My *wrath* shall be kindled against this place, and shall *not* be quenched" (verses 16-17). Their allegiance had been transferred from the true God to that which was false, spurious, unholy, and unrighteous, completely contrary to all they had been taught. Therefore they had become totally intolerable to God.

Professing Christians today have transferred their allegiance to that which is abominable to God. That which secures the devotion of those who claim to be His disciples is equally intolerable to God. It may be a bottle or it may be a motorboat, or a motorcycle. Or it may just be some tickets to the stock car races. It may be a deck of cards, or it may be the "boob tube" in the corner of the living room. It may be a carton of king-size, filter-tipped cancer sticks, or the back seat of a parked car. It may be the waxed floor with the jazz combo, or it may be the adulation of a gilded society. It may be the social sewage of Hollywood, which has finally destroyed the moral fiber of the nation, or it may be simply a life given over to *getting* rather than *giving*. It may be a vile, vicious, Satanic, backbiting tongue, which tears and destroys, backstabbing those who are trying to live for God, or to preach His Word; criticizing everybody and everything which does not cater to the personal whims of a selfish, self-righteous, and sophisticated church membership. Whatever it is that commands the concern, the devotion, and interest of any person who names the name of Christ today, it has the curse of God upon it, and it is time to flee from it.

In the face of this impending doom, there is one note of mercy. "But," says the Lord to Josiah, "Because thine heart was tender, and thou hast humbled thyself," there will be a fifteen-year postponement, "and thine eyes shall not see all the evil which I will bring upon this place" (verses 18-20).

If one tenderhearted man, humbling himself sincerely before God, could postpone the judgment of a nation, what could God do if an entire congregation would humble itself before the Lord? If *one* could postpone for fifteen years, *all* could avert the disaster entirely. Yet it is almost impossible to find even a Josiah who will get down in the dust today.

We would do well to read again the third chapter of Jonah, when a similar message of disaster was presented to that wicked city of Nineveh. "And God saw their works, that they *turned* from their evil way; and God repented of the evil, that He had said that He would do unto them; and *He did it not*" (Jonah 3:10).

Resolution

Josiah did everything that he could do in order to bring the people into a right relationship with God. He gathered the people together and gave them the truth as it was stated in the book. Apparently he read it to them himself, which was quite unusual. They could hardly fail to grasp the solemn significance of this matter, when the king himself took the initiative. Then the king set up the covenant, subscribing to it himself, and making it possible for the people to subscribe to it. It was no superficial endorsement which the king was requiring of them. They were to enter into it "with all their heart and all their soul" (2 Kings 23:3). They were to *"walk* after the LORD," they were to *"keep* His commandments . . . testimonies . . . statutes . . . [and] to *perform* the words of this covenant." This certainly goes farther and deeper than most of our "do it a little better" sort of propositions which we set before the members today. "And *all* the people *stood* to the covenant." We would be astounded if we could get a fourth of the people even to listen to such a covenant today, much less stand to it. The majority of our present-day "joiners" would be opposed to such a covenant, if they were to discover that it had been presented to the church.

Josiah did not ask them to give their approval and agree to the fact that it was a well-stated resolution which should be published in the denominational paper. The demand was that it not only be adopted, but carried out, by everyone standing there. Performance is the prerequisite to peace and blessing. From that point on everything depended upon the genuineness and sincerity of the people, in that to which they had taken their stand. Josiah could not provide that for anyone but himself.

3. THE REFORMATION FOR REVIVAL

Repudiation—the Negative Aspect

The approval of the covenant was followed by a tremendous housecleaning. The rubbish, the trash, that which was false and spurious had to go before true worship could be established. The groves, the idols, the altars, the vessels, all had to be destroyed, and the false priests excommunicated. "And he brought out the grove from the house of the LORD . . . and stamped it small to powder" (verse 6). There was to be no transfer of the unholy to "higher purposes" and no "taking the best from each" and uniting them for godly service. There has to be a clean sweep when we do business with God. Too many are taking their trash from the old carnal life along with them, and then we wonder why God is not blessing the activities. It took seventeen long verses to describe this cleansing program. "He broke down the houses of the Sodomites" (verse 7) and disposed of the priests who had led the people astray. There was a complete removal of those who had taught error and set a bad example. Such procedure would be most desirable in some of our educational institutions today.

Mountains of rubbish need to be swept out of our lives today, out of our homes, and even out of our churches, if we expect to enjoy the blessing of God upon our worship and work. Our prayers and programs will continue to be futile and fruitless until we start where Josiah started — with the wide broom.

Reclamation — the Positive Aspect

Following the cleanup operation is the reestablishment of the passover. It can be said to their credit that, as long as they were indulging in idolatry, they did not hypocritically pretend to carry out this divinely established observance. First, the false must be removed and displaced before the true can properly replace it. It took only three verses to describe the setting up of this memorial. It does not take long to get going in the right direction, if God can get us away from the old carnalities. "Moreover the workers with familiar spirits . . . wizards . . . idols . . . and all the abominations . . . did Josiah *put away,* that he might *perform* the words of the law" (verse 24). When will we ever learn that we must "put away" before we can "perform"? Having eliminated that which was abominable to God, the king sought to lead them in true worship and devotion to God. This was all that he could do, but it was enough to bring revival from Heaven, and to avert the judgment of God, *if it were the real thing.*

No greater tribute could be paid to any man than was paid to Josiah. "And like unto him was there no king before him, that turned to the LORD *with all his heart,* and *with all his soul,* and *with all his might,* according to *all* the law of Moses; neither after him arose there any like him" (verse 25). There could be no question about the absolute earnestness and sincerity of that man.

Notwithstanding — how that word stands out, in letters of burning fire. "Notwithstanding the LORD turned *not* from the fierceness of His great wrath, wherewith His anger was kindled against Judah" (verse 26). Why did He not turn? What more could Josiah do? Despite all the favorable pursuits and proper preparations, there was no *real revival*. Where did Josiah fail? He did not fail; it was the people who failed. Josiah went all out for God, but the people did not go half way. They *stood* but they did not *walk*. They *professed* but they did not *perform*. They *approved* but did not *keep* His commandments. The king must have been thrilled when all the people stood, because it was voluntary — he had not threatened reprisal for those who did not conform. Nevertheless it was all superficial, a mere outward demonstration without any inward conviction or purpose to back it up. *Notwithstanding* — there was no revival. How tragic!

Many pastors today are ashamed to find that, even when people walk the aisles with tears, they cannot help wondering — is this the real thing? Will there be a new devotion to God and to His house when the campaign is over? Will there be an increase in attendance at all the services, an increase in tithes and offerings, a new enthusiasm in witnessing for Jesus, which will result in many more genuine professions of faith on the part of the lost? Or shall we expect to be all settled back into the old rut, with the same faithful remnant within two weeks? Would to God that all the people would *stand,* and *really* mean it, and then go out to *perform*. God grant it, before this country becomes totally pagan. "For when they shall *say,* Peace and safety; then sudden destruction cometh upon them" (1 Thessalonians 5:3).

EPILOGUE

ARE WE GETTING THE JOB DONE?

A very striking article appeared in one of our journals recently, written by Dr. Rush Bush, a contemporary professor of preaching in one of our Baptist seminaries. It goes right to the heart of Biblical preaching under the title, "Are You Sure You 'Preach The Word'?" If space would permit, it would be profitable to include the entire article, but we shall have to confine ourselves to some pertinent quotes. Dr. Bush starts off by saying:

> I have never met a Southern Baptist preacher who did not claim to be a "Bible preacher." [There are some.] Let's omit those ministers who never find time to study (thus at best producing devotional drivel every service) and ask whether or not even the conscientious *student* of the Word is really a *preacher* of the Word.

The professor then goes on to show that even though topical preaching may be Biblical, in the sense that it coincides with the content of the Bible, and may seem to appeal to the "needs" of the

165

listener, it is not really preaching the Word. He then says:

Paul unequivocally affirms that Scripture has been written "for our learning" (Romans 15:4). That "learning" results in a practical application for us, but are such results to be the focus of our preaching?

A few years ago I made a limited personal survey to find out the level of Bible content knowledge in churches in three states. My conclusions are not scientific or infallible, but I found a poverty of factual information about the Bible. Walking into an adult Sunday school class and asking the members to interpret a passage of Scripture in its theological context is normally useless. Either you get no response or else you get a very shallow response.

I used to think this fact was due to an unwillingness to learn on the part of modern church members. I now see it as a direct result of a weak pulpit ministry. Our sermons have been Biblical, yes, but *we are not preaching the Word.*

Scripture was written to teach us. We need to be taught. All Scripture is God-breathed and it is theologically and ethically useful to equip God's people for good works (2 Timothy 3:16-17). . . . All of it is useful for equipping the saints to live their daily life.

So then, in the presence of God and of Jesus Christ (as Paul expresses it), and in view of His appearing and His kingdom, *preach the Word.* That means taking a Biblical passage and *reproducing the message of the passage in your sermon.*

By far the best way to do that is consistently to follow a Biblical pattern such as preaching through a book. . . . God will use His Word to accomplish

His purpose. Our task is to preach it, *preach all of it*. . . . We are to preach the Word, not just *from* the Word.

Dr. Bush does not eliminate topical or textual preaching altogether, and sees advantages in such preaching, but his main thrust is expository preaching. So he concludes with this pungent and practical counsel:

Take the Biblical narrative and make it come alive in your pulpit. Take the psalm and use it to offer praise to God. Take that doctrinal passage and explain it in all of its fullness. Take that prophet and deliver his message to your people today.

Surely God speaks clearly. We need not be so concerned to *improve on God's Word.* Somehow we think people themselves can never apply Biblical teaching to life, but the problem is *they don't understand what the Biblical teaching is.* Yes, I clearly spell out practical applications in my sermons, but that part of the message should be so self-explanatory that it needs only a hint. The bulk of the message should be in content exposition. Let God speak to the people. *Let God do the "preaching."* Let us proclaim His Word in context, with clarity, and with power. [Italics mine.]

It would be well for all of us to ponder the question which Dr. Bush raises. Are we really sure we are preaching the Word? I have heard sermons which purportedly followed the counsel given here, but still did not *really* preach the Word. The hearers were not indoctrinated in the passage under consideration, and did not know any more about that Scripture than they did before. The preacher did not "Let God do the 'preaching.'"

Though he does not deal with the matter of "redeeming the time," when it comes to expository preaching I am confident that Dr. Bush would be perfectly frank to say that the man who purposes in his heart to really "preach the Word" will have to make up his mind to be diligent in the matter of dedicated preparation. So we need to think about:

THE MATTER OF SELF-DISCIPLINE

Through the years the writer has engaged in a lot of "shop talk" with other preachers. When it got right down to the nitty-gritty some of them adroitly changed the subject. In some cases it was useless to continue, due to an insufficient understanding of the subject of homiletics. Then there were those who frankly admitted that expository preaching could be beneficial but they just did not have the desire to do it. Probably the majority agreed that it was un-doubtedly the most profitable type of ministry, but it just took more time to prepare, and thus they could not see their way clear to give the time required to become proficient at it.

There is so much emphasis upon counseling, ad-ministration, and personality adjustments, etc., with many other pressures, that many men have allowed the pulpit ministry to take a back seat. I think that the theological schools are at least partially to blame for this. The curriculum in most of them will be full of courses in psychology, sociology, pastoral counseling, programing, church administration, and similar pursuits. Then note how little is offered in the realm of homiletics, in comparsion. Many of the courses which go under the heading of "preaching" are taken up with the history of preaching, denominational emphasis, the order of worship, pulpit decorum, attendance building, utilizing music in the worship service, invitations, children's services, etc., and never get right down to the matter of preaching. This is not to say that we should not be informed in these aforementioned matters, but not to the exclusion of the most important thing.

I once asked a brilliant young seminary graduate if there was a major emphasis upon expository preaching in the seminary courses where he attended. He said that he was not qualified to answer the question since *he did not take any courses in homiletics.* What a travesty!

Certainly the most important thing for the preacher is to have a solid and comprehensive grasp of the Scriptures in the vernacular—the English Bible for us. Second only to that he should be well versed in the realm of homiletics. The science of preparing and delivering sermons is absolutely essential to an influential ministry. To *know* the Word ourselves, and to *impart* it to others, is the main business of the God-called preacher. Let everything else take second place to that.

Since preaching is that important, and expository preaching is obviously the most beneficial to both preacher and congregation, at least some emphasis should be given to it each year. If the reader feels that he is not well prepared in the realm of homiletics, we would urge him to read at least some of the books which will receive special commendation in this volume.

If he wishes really to "preach the Word," let him make up his mind that he will discipline himself to that end. He must learn to say *No* and mean it. It is not easy, but it can be done.

Every man will have to arrange a schedule that suits his "peculiar style of awkwardness" and stay with it. The writer has found the following to be the most satisfactory procedure in present-day circumstances. Maybe it will prove suggestive.

In earlier years I got up between five and six o'clock in the morning and went immediately to the study. When breakfast was ready I went to the kitchen and conducted family devotions, ate a light breakfast, and then back to the study. Apart from natural diversions I would stay there until eleven or eleven-thirty. Then I would dress and shave and go to the post office, after which I went by the church. (My study was usually in the home.) In later years I did not rise so early.

After lunch I would read the paper and take a nap. No paper, no radio, no media news or information until after lunch. Then the rest of the day was taken up with correspondence, administration, or pastoral ministries. Most of the personal evangelism had to be done after supper, since people were rarely home in the daytime. This was the regular· procedure Tuesday through Saturday.

Sunday morning I went immediately to the study and prayed and meditated over the message until time to start out for Sunday school. Sometimes folks would ask: "Say, did you hear so-and-so on the radio? Or, did you see such-and-such on television? Or, did you read that article in the paper?" My answer was always negative. There was no time for that. I always said that the ideal situation would be to step into the pulpit without having said a word to any human being. That, of course, is impractical, no matter how desirable. If you want to be at your best when you stand before your congregation, give God all the time possible, to have yourself in readiness to "preach the Word." That in turn leads to:

THE MATTER OF CONGREGATIONAL DISCIPLINE

I think that most men feel that they could not, or dare not, set up such a schedule. The demands are so great that they feel frustrated and condemned if they do not measure up to them. A man thinks that if he closets himself away with God like that he will be castigated by his people, and not without reason. Generally speaking, the people who make up our congregations have never been more demanding or more inconsiderate than they are today. Thousands of men are leaving the pastorate because of it.

However, I believe the man who leaves because he feels that he cannot endure it any longer, will do so with a great sense of satisfaction in the knowledge that he tried to create the right attitude on the part of his congregation, concerning the most important matter of the pastorate.

On the other hand, I firmly believe that if a pastor goes about it in the right way, taking time and patiently showing the people that this request is for their benefit as well as that of the pastor, he can develop a cooperative spirit on the part of the people. It will take time.

Only this morning I heard a pastor of a church in another state, which numbers about two thousand five hundred members in the congregation, say that he faced and surmounted this problem. When he went to that pastorate about sixteen years ago he said that he felt that his words were coming back into his own face, as though he were in a wind tunnel. He made his plea to his people to help him preserve the morning hours for study, and he would promise them he would never come before them unprepared to preach God's Word. After several years of cooperation in this matter, a deacon stood before the congregation and reminded them of this plea which the pastor had made, and said, "I have heard our pastor preach more often than anyone here, and he has never failed us. He has been well prepared every time he stood in the pulpit." That church averages about eight hundred people at each of the two Sunday morning services, about seven hundred on Sunday evening and four hundred on Wednesday evening.

Obviously there will be days when everything seems to go wrong. Hectic days when so much presses down on a man that he cannot get near his study, or could not concentrate if he did. But if a man will stick to his schedule just as often as humanly possible, it will pay off, and the congregation will know it, whether or not they fully appreciate it. Do not say it *cannot* be done until you have tried desperately hard.

RESOURCE MATERIAL

From the Homiletical Standpoint

From 1910 to 1940 there have been, to our knowledge, only five books written, which deal exclusively with expository preaching.

The Art of Exposition, by Harry Jeffs, 1910

Expository Preaching, Plans and Methods, by F. B. Meyer, 1910

How To Prepare an Expository Sermon, by Harold E. Knott, 1930

Expository Preaching, by Ames Montgomery, 1939

Expository Preaching, by Jefferson D. Ray, 1940

The volume entitled *Preaching,* by G. Campbell Morgan (1937), is not confined to expository preaching, though he probably had that in mind when he wrote it, because he excelled in that realm. All of the foregoing have points of value, though most of them are out of print.

In *The Theory of Preaching* Dr. Austin Phelps gives an excellent discussion of the "proposition,"

175

devoting about eighty-three pages to that one element of the sermon. Dr. Whitesell also has a practical word to say on that matter in his *Evangelistic Preaching and the Old Testament.*

From 1952 to the present time there have apparently been only four books devoted exclusively to the matter of expository preaching.

Expository Preaching for Today, by Andrew W. Blackwood, 1953

Principles of Expository Preaching, by Merrill F. Unger, 1955

Power in Expository Preaching, by Faris D. Whitesell, 1954

He Expounded, by Douglas M. White, 1952 (out of print)

There is a multitude of books in the general category of homiletics. I would urge every preacher to try and secure the following titles, most of which are out of print. They will be very helpful in all types of preaching.

The Art of Illustrating Sermons, by Dawson C. Bryan (provides excellent instruction in the use of illustrations and selection of topics).

The Art of Biblical Preaching, by Faris D. Whitesell (a "must" in homiletics).

Preaching from the Bible, by Andrew W. Blackwood.

The Work of the Ministry, by W. H. Griffith Thomas.

The Preacher and His Preaching, by W. B. Riley.

From the Exegetical Standpoint

When preparing to launch a series of consecutive expositions the writer has always tried to secure separate volumes written by a scholar who has majored on that particular book of the Bible. When a man concentrates on one particular portion he usually has something very valuable to offer. For instance, when preaching through the book of Acts, I secured books by G. Campbell Morgan (in my judgment the best volume ever written on Acts), H. A. Ironside, J. C. McCauley, and two volumes by Herschel Ford. There were other sources which I consulted, but these proved the most fruitful. I derived much more information from these volumes than from the full Bible commentaries.

Other volumes which have been most helpful in sermon preparation, first for Old Testament studies are: *Old Testament History* by Alfred Edersheim (2 volumes); several volumes by H. A. Ironside; and some by Campbell Morgan. Volumes by F. B. Meyer, William Taylor, Arthur Pink, Kyle Yates, and Alan Redpath. In both Old and New Testaments, F. W. Krummacher, Griffith Thomas, C. H. Mackintosh.

Of the volumes which offer a broader coverage there is none better than *Word Studies in the Greek New Testament* by Kenneth S. Wuest. These volumes are a must for every expositor. *The New Testament in 26 Translations* is also valuable, and is a time-saver. Possession of that volume should not rule out the use of other translations however.

Two one-volume commentaries on the whole Bible are very useful. *The Wycliffe Bible Commentary* and the *Matthew Henry Commentary. Jamieson, Fawcett and Brown,* in the unabridged six-volume set, provides valuable insights, though some portions are disappointing. There are many other commentaries, of course, but each man must decide what suits his style. It is wise to look over these larger commentaries before making a purchase.

LIMITED BIBLIOGRAPHY

Alexander, J. W., *Thoughts on Preaching*, New York: Scribner, 1860.

Black, James, *The Mystery of Preaching*, New York: Revell, 1924, 1935.

Blackwood, Andrew W., *Expository Preaching for Today*, New York: Abingdon-Cokesbury, 1953.

_____, *Preaching from the Bible*, New York: Abingdon-Cokesbury, 1941.

_____, *The Preparation of Sermons*, New York: Abingdon-Cokesbury, 1938.

Bonar, Andrew A., *The Biography of Robert Murray M'Cheyne*, Grand Rapids: Michigan: Zondervan, (reprint) 1950.

Brastow, Louis, *The Work of the Preacher*, Boston: Pilgrim Press, 1914.

Breed, David R., *Preparing to Preach*, New York: George H. Doran, 1911. (Try Harper Brothers.)

Broadus, John A., *The Preparation and Delivery of Sermons*, New York: George H. Doran, 1870.

_____, *The History of Preaching*, New York: A. C. Armstrong and Son, 1876.

Brooks, Phillips, *Lectures on Preaching,* New York: E. P. Dutton, 1877.

Brown, Northcutt & Clinard, *Steps to a Sermon,* Nashville, Broadman, 1963.

Burrell, David J., *The Sermon—Its Construction and Delivery,* New York: Revell, 1913.

Bryan, Dawson., *The Art of Illustrating Sermons,* New York: Abingdon-Cokesbury, 1938.

Bush, Rush, "Are You Sure You 'Preach the Word' "? *The Baptist Program,* Nashville, Tennessee, October 1974.

Coltman, William G., *The Cathedral of Christian Truth,* Findlay, Ohio: Fundamental Truth Publishers, 1944.

Chappell, Clovis G., *Anointed to Preach,* New York: Abingdon-Cokesbury, 1951.

Dabney, Robert Lewis, *Lectures on Sacred Rhetoric,* Richmond, Virginia: Presbyterian Committee of Publication, 1870.

Dargan, Edwin Charles, *The Art of Preaching in the Light of Its History,* Nashville, Tennessee: Sunday School Board of the Southern Baptist Convention, 1922.

Evans, J. Ellwood, "Expository Preaching," *Bibliotheca Sacra,* Dallas: Dallas Theological Seminary, January 1954.

Evans, William, *How to Prepare Sermons and Gospel Addresses,* Chicago: Bible Institute Colportage Association, 1913, now Moody Press.

_____, *The Book Method of Bible Study,* Chicago: Bible Institute Colportage Association, 1915, now Moody Press.

Hall, John, *God's Word Through Preaching,* New York: Dodd, Mead, 1875.

Jeffs, H., *The Art of Exposition,* Boston: Pilgrim Press, 1910.

Jones, Bob, Jr., *How to Improve Your Preaching,* New York: Revell, 1945.

Jones, Ilion T., *Principles and Practice of Preaching,* New York: Abingdon Press, 1956.

Jowett, John Henry, *The Preacher—His Life and Work,* New York: George H. Doran, 1912.

Kennedy, Gerald, *His Word Through Preaching,* New York: Harper & Brothers, 1947.

Kerr, Hugh Thompson, *Preaching in the Early Church,* New York: Revell, 1942.

Kidder, D. P., *A Treatise on Homiletics,* New York: Hunt and Eaton, 1864.

Knott, Harold E., *How to Prepare an Expository Sermon,* Cincinnati, Ohio: The Standard Press, 1930.

Lenski, R. C. H., *The Sermon—Its Homiletical Construction,* Columbus, Ohio: Lutheran Book Concern, 1927.

Lloyd-Jones, D. Martin, *Preaching and Preachers,* Grand Rapids, Michigan: Zondervan, 1971.

Macaulay, J. C., *A Devotional Commentary on the Acts of the Apostles,* Grand Rapids, Michigan: William B. Eerdmans, 1946.

McCartney, C. E., *Preaching Without Notes,* New York: Abingdon-Cokesbury, 1946.

Meyer, F. B., *Expository Preaching, Plans and Methods,* New York: George H. Doran, 1910.

Montgomery, R. Ames, *Expository Preaching,* New York: Revell, 1939.

Morgan, G. Campbell, *Preaching,* New York: Revell, 1937.

Pattison, T. Harwood, *The Making of the Sermon,* Philadelphia: Judson Press, 1898.

Petry, Ray C., *No Uncertain Sound,* Philadelphia: The Westminster Press, 1948.

Phelps, Austin, *The Theory of Preaching,* New York: Scribner, 1890.

Pierson, Arthur T., *Knowing the Scriptures,* New York: Gospel Publishing House, 1910.

Ray, Jeff D., *Expository Preaching,* Grand Rapids, Michigan: Zondervan, 1940.

Riley, W. B., *The Preacher and His Preaching,*
Wheaton, Illinois: Sword of the Lord, 1948.

Roach, C. C., *Preaching Values in the Bible,*
Louisville, Kentucky: Cloister Press, 1946.

Robertson, A. T., *Studies in the Epistle of James,*
New York: George H. Doran, 1915.

Roddy, Clarence Stonelyn, editor, *We Prepare and
Preach,* Chicago: Moody Press, 1959.

Smith, Wilbur M., *Profitable Bible Study,* Boston:
W. A. Wilde, 1939; Grand Rapids, Michigan:
Baker Book House.

Spurgeon, C. H., *Lectures to My Students,* London:
Passmore and Alabaster, 1877. (Out of business.)

Taylor, W. M., *The Ministry of the Word,*
Randolph and Company, 1876.

Thomas, W. H. Griffith, *The Work of the Ministry,*
London: Hodder and Stoughton, 1910.

Torrey, R. A. *What the Bible Teaches,* New York:
Revell, 1898.

Unger, Merrill F., *Principles of Expository
Preaching,* Grand Rapids, Michigan: Zondervan,
1955.

Vinet, A., *The Theory of Preaching,* New York:
Ivison and Phinney, 1855.

Wagner, Don M., *The Expository Method of
G. Campbell Morgan,* New York: Revell, 1957.

Wayland, Francis, *Letters on the Ministry of the Gospel,* Boston: Gould and Lincoln, 1863.

Whitesell, Faris D., *Evangelistic Preaching and the Old Testament,* Chicago: Moody Press, 1947.

_____, *The Art of Biblical Preaching,* Grand Rapids, Michigan: Zondervan, 1950.

_____, *Power in Expository Preaching,* New York: Revell, 1953.

_____, and Perry, Lloyd M., *Variety in Your Preaching,* New York: Revell, 1954.

White, Douglas M., *The Sufferings of the Saints,* Chicago: Moody Press, 1947.

_____, *He Expounded,* Chicago: Moody Press, 1952.

Wuest, Kenneth S., *Mark in the Greek New Testament,* Grand Rapids, Michigan: William B. Eerdmans, 1950.

DOCUMENTARY INDEX

185

INDEX OF SCRIPTURE REFERENCES

189

4241